Lord Gladwyn

Chairman of the "Campaign for Europe",
formerly British Ambassador to the
United Nations and to France

Europe
After
De Gaulle

Foreword by
Vera Micheles Dean

TAPLINGER PUBLISHING COMPANY
NEW YORK

First published in the United States in 1969 by
Taplinger Publishing Co., Inc.
29 East Tenth Street
New York, New York 10003

SBN 8008-2520-9

Library of Congress Catalog Card Number 70–86972

Author of

THE EUROPEAN IDEA

HALF-WAY TO 1984

"*Flectere si nequeo superos Acheronta movebo*"

Printed in Great Britain

Contents

Acknowledgments

My thanks are due to Mrs Annette Morgan, for her invaluable and accurate research; to Mrs Charles Pickthorn for proof-reading; to my daughter, Vanessa Thomas, for the Index; to my superb secretary, Mrs Irene Hunter, for coping with my dreadful MS.; and to all those knowledgeable friends, academic, journalistic and other, who gave me excellent advice but might not necessarily, I feel, wish to be associated with all my conclusions.

"... I have thought it proper to represent things as they are in real truth, rather than as they are imagined ..."
Niccolo Machiavelli
(The Prince, XV).

Foreword

NOW THAT General Charles de Gaulle has relinquished the presidency of France by a peaceful withdrawal from the political scene which does credit to the rule of a military leader over a nation whose democracy he did not destroy, this lively controversial book by Lord Gladwyn, chairman of the "Campaign for Europe," and former British Ambassador to France and to the United Nations, acquires fresh interest. For the world community will have the opportunity of discovering whether, with the General no longer in command, France will follow a foreign policy significantly different from his.

Lord Gladwyn eloquently contends that the French leader, whom his admirers—and even some of his critics—regard as the architect of France's postwar revival and as a pioneer in peaceful decolonization both of Vietnam and of French possessions in North Africa—notably Algeria—was a stubborn obstacle to what might be called the internationalization of Europe. In reality, was "le Grand Charles" merely a stubborn "Nay-sayer" to all intervention in Europe by non-European powers—notably Britain and the United States—as contended by his critics? Or did he represent a genuine sentiment on the part not only of many Frenchmen, but also of other Europeans in favor of creating a European Community, friendly both with Washington on the West, and the USSR on the East—but without becoming subservient to either of the great multiracial giants of our times?

What is often forgotten, in this international and intercontinental debate, is that de Gaulle's great contribution has been the restoration of a militarily defeated, politically confused and economically shattered France—if not to the *grandeur* to which the General aspired, then, and most important for the future both of France and of the world, to a point where it can again play a significant role in world affairs—not as an imperial power in the Napoleonic sense, a role it has left far behind—but as what could prove a valuable balance-wheel between the two great empires of our time, the United States and the USSR. Moreover, as Henry Brandon has wisely pointed out in *The Saturday Review* of May 24, 1969, while most of Europe's capitals favor Britain's entrance into Europe from a political point of view, "Economically speaking . . . there is much less of a consensus, and gradually we will come to see that de Gaulle was not the only troublemaker. For many, he was a convenient excuse."

If Britain—as well as the United States—both of whom de Gaulle, in spite of their wartime contributions to victory over Nazi Germany, regarded as intruders into Europe—can bring themselves to understand this psychological problem, it may prove possible to create, with France's active participation, a more viable and closely knit Europe which could hold its own between the two giants—the United States and the USSR—and conceivably bring to an end the postwar confrontation between the two Germanies.

VERA MICHELES DEAN

Introduction

IN THIS small book I analyse, as objectively as I can, the development of the European policy of the French Government under President de Gaulle and attempt to assess the consequences if, by any ill chance, it should be continued by his successors. What exactly was this policy? What did it have in common with the European policy of the Fourth French Republic? How successful was it from the point of view of France? What effect did it have on European unity, on Franco-British relations, and what were its implications for the maintenance of peace? By "European policy" I mean, in a general way, the attitude of the French Government during this period towards the growth, and possible enlargement of the European Economic Community; the eventual construction of a European Political Community; the rightful place, as the French Government saw it, of France in Europe; and the ultimate aims which that Government apparently pursued.

Each of these aspects deserves a long and scholarly volume, and indeed one of over 2,000 pages on the general subject has recently appeared; but the present work is more in the nature of an essay designed to assist those who cannot spare the time to make a deep study of a problem which most of us nevertheless feel to be of the utmost importance to this country and, indeed, to the entire world. Whether Western Europe comes together during the next few years in any real sense, or not, is something which must affect, for better or worse, the relationship between the Super-Powers and consequently that balance of power on which our present "peace" precariously rests. And, whatever our own views may be, it is largely on the

policy of France that the great issue hangs. For France
is so situated, and indeed her whole history has been
such, that anything in the way of a complete organic
entity in Western Europe is, literally, inconceivable
without her. Such an entity may never emerge. Some
may dispute the need to form it anyhow. Others
would say that it cannot, in practice, be formed without the United Kingdom. But all must admit that, if
it ever is to be fully achieved it must, in the long run,
be with willing French participation.

This short examination of Gaullist policy cannot,
I fear, be unprejudiced. In my book *The European
Idea*, and in many speeches and articles I have, since
my retirement from the Foreign Service in 1960,
severely criticized the European policy of de Gaulle.
But I doubt whether this precludes me from at least
attempting a fair analysis, though it will certainly
colour my summing-up. Besides, we must always remember that, as he himself says in his book *Vers
l'Armée de métier*[1] "cunning must be used [in dealing
with the enemy] in order to make him believe that one
is where one is not, that one wants something quite
different from what one does," or again, in *Le Fil de
l'Epée*[2] "The man of action is hardly imaginable without a strong admixture of egoism, pride, toughness
and deceit [*ruse*]."

What de Gaulle has said in public, therefore, on
"Europe" need not always be taken completely literally, but must be judged in the context of the political
situation existing at the time. In my analysis I am,
naturally, dependent on the text rather than on the

[1] *The Army of the Future*, Hutchinson, p. 122.
[2] *The Edge of the Sword*, Faber and Faber, 1960.

presumptive motive; but in my comment I shall make my own interpretation. What we can all do is to attempt to understand not only his mentality but that of the millions of Frenchmen who, until fairly recently, thought that, for France at any rate, his European policy was just the thing. Perhaps, after reading this book, the reader will feel that "*tout comprendre, c'est tout pardonner*," a motto which, needless to say, is hardly one which the General would make his own! Or the reader may even arrive at the conclusion that there is nothing to forgive.

The one essential thing is thought. How should the British best react as a nation to attempts to unite Europe without them? Do they really want, on political grounds, to form part of a new Western European entity? And, unless they have that desire and that will, have they any chance of preventing the formation of Europe without Great Britain and its inclusion in some new union dominated, by the very force of things, by America? These are the questions which confront every inhabitant of these islands at the present time. It is no good drifting along in the hope that the problem will solve itself, for drift will only carry the British further and further out into the Atlantic and they may shortly reach the point of no return. The decision will, in other words, have been taken without any conscious or collective effort on their part. What will happen on the mainland of Europe will be anybody's guess, but their own future will have already been determined. They will have become a satellite of the United States, happy enough, perhaps, in their quite subordinate role, but with little or no say in the formation of policy.

It is arguable that a supra-national "Europe," as originally conceived, or even as modified in the light of recent events, cannot now be formed; that the principle of nationalism, as advocated and indeed to some extent imposed by General de Gaulle, has won the day; and that, short of chaos, the choice is consequently between a French-directed European "Confederation" and an American-directed "Atlantic Community"—unless the West Germans prefer to do a direct deal with the Soviet Union, in which unlikely case the continental Western European democracies will all probably fall under Russian, rather than American influence. What the chances of such various developments are the reader will probably be unable to estimate, or rather his guess will probably be as good as anybody else's. But what he should at least try to do is to grasp, in the light of the evidence, what the effect of French European policy has recently been and what results it may be expected to achieve if it is continued. For it is only in the light of this that he will then be able to make up his mind on the desirability and, indeed, on the political effects of further efforts on the part of the British to join what is nearly always referred to by this "nation of shop-keepers" as the "Common Market."

Here I should like to say a word about the apparent views of the international student movement which can hardly be ignored since, whatever older people may think of it, it did at least spark off something equivalent to a minor revolution in France and may even, therefore, be said to have affected the policy which is the subject of our present enquiry. Evidently, not all young people think the same things or approve the same policies. But there does seem to be a feeling among many of the educated or partly educated youth in all our countries that "new structures" are needed and that in any case there is not, and should not be, any impediment to the circulation throughout Europe of men and ideas, even if, as in the Middle Ages, such men and ideas bear no strong allegiance to any particular nation.

Many of these young men and women may be anarchists, seeing in the total disruption of our industrialized society the only hope of the future. But I prefer to believe that the majority of the younger generation are in favour of a new type of society that will somehow emerge from the old. Whether they will come out in favour of a particular "European" structure is doubtful. Maybe they cannot or do not wish to formulate their ideas too definitely. Maybe they are suspicious of any "structure" involving governments and expert members of the economic and political "establishments." But no "structures" can in practice be formed in our industrialized societies without the participation of such persons and there should be a possibility of capturing the active support of young people for a new, democratic European set-up of some kind provided only that it is democratic in the sense of giving greater power to the so-called "Parliament of Europe." And surely there is a danger that unless the opinion of young people develops in this direction some may yet fall for the kind of nationalism that their elders knew as Fascism?

The men who launched the existing "Europe," insofar as it does exist, are now mostly in their sixties or seventies. If "Europe" is ever going to be formed a further impetus will be required, and this is only likely to come from those now in their thirties or forties. No great cause has ever triumphed without enthusiasm and brains, and the latter are certainly not lacking. But democratic governments will only react to popular pressure. If they feel that the bulk of the electorate, including the younger members, are quite happy in their limited national states and do not perceive how much better off they would be, both economically and politically, by uniting, they will probably not take the "great leap forward" inherent in acceptance of any supra-national objectives, however minimal to start off with. But if they feel that the majority of their supporters tend to equate national government with import controls, or heavy unemployment or even, on the best hypothesis, with "Stop, Go," then it is possible that they will willingly accept a system whereby, subject to a measure of Parliamentary control, certain decisions are taken in a central place by a form of majority vote, after having been for long discussed between national representatives and "neutral" experts.

There is a theory that the Communities only advanced as far as they did because until about 1962 the curve of European production was rising rapidly and no strong stresses and strains consequently presented themselves. Equally, as soon as they did, the Communities began to get into trouble and "national" forces raised their ugly heads. On this theory, which is no doubt only partially valid, the difficulties which afflicted the Communities from about 1962 onwards were in some way due to the fact that the populations concerned did not attribute their increased prosperity to the machine which, to a very considerable extent, had been responsible for it. But on the other hand it may be said that the essential reason why the Communities ever came into existence at all was because of the appalling memories of the Second World War and the necessity of ending that suicidal national rivalry which, to all seeming, had occasioned it. So it may be that if the general economic situation in Western Europe gets notably worse—and it very well may—the thoughts of many will turn to revolutionary proposals, or if not revolutionary then at any rate unprecedented.

The acceptance, for instance, of a common Community Budget, based on the enormous income deriving not only from the agricultural levies but also from Customs duties generally, could be used with powerful effect to combat the effects of a slump, or any breakdown of the international monetary system. And, indeed, once we arrive at this point there will be evident need for a common European monetary policy. Desperate situations, in other words, could produce desperate remedies. What we ought all to do, surely, is to prepare for a rather revolutionary situation and, if possible, to create, or at least to imagine, machinery by means of which new ideologies can be canalized without too much damage to the ancient national structures of the various nation states of Europe.

Are such prospects just the fond imaginings of enthusiasts, of self-seeking "experts" doomed, as de Gaulle says, and thinks, to absolute frustration? Is the only practical alternative the ruthless pursuit of national policies ending up in the exercise of leadership by one nation and the consequent formation of what the ex-President of France calls a "Confederation" but which others might go so far as to call a new kind of Empire—whether it be French or German? And is it true that, should all such efforts at union fail, the only future for our ancient lands is abject surrender to the will of Russia or America? This is the subject of our study. Let us therefore ring up the curtain on Paris in early May 1958 and on the state of "Europe" at that moment.

1

The Gaullist Inheritance

THE BACKGROUND of the French Government's position in early May 1958 as regards the creation of "Europe" was as follows. The Fourth French Republic, whose establishment at the end of 1945 more or less coincided with the voluntary withdrawal from the scene of General de Gaulle, had pursued a fairly consistent and not unsuccessful foreign policy. This was largely due to the fact that between 1944 and 1954 the Foreign Ministry was almost continuously occupied alternately by two members of the same party (the Mouvement Republicain Populaire), Georges Bidault and Robert Schuman. Since about 1948, when it became apparent that the "traditional" French policy of a break-up of the Reich was impossible of achievement, one major objective of the French Government, not shared, of course, by the Communists and the extreme Right, had been entirely clear. This was the formation, in Western Europe, of some kind of European Union, more or less "federal" in structure, of which an essential member, apart from France, was Germany, or rather West Germany. The presence in such a Union of the United Kingdom also, if not absolutely essential, was highly desirable, but only if she accepted certain supranational obligations. Pro-British though many of the French Cabinet Ministers during this period undoubtedly were, vivid though the recollection of "liberation" by British troops, particularly in the North, undoubtedly was, this was something which was regarded as a sort of touchstone. For unless she was really "in" Europe Britain could hardly be relied upon not to pursue some policy which might yet again result in her being able to pull her own chestnuts out of the fire while France herself got badly burnt. The reasons for this attitude lay deep in French history and their validity would probably, in practice, have been accepted by any French Government during this period—even by a French Communist government, if such a thing had been conceivable. They had to do with the sad struggles over the centuries between the Gauls and the Teutons and, more immediately, with the traumatic shock in 1940, never really understood by the British, of the total defeat and four-year occupation of France.

Immediately after the war de Gaulle was in charge for some eighteen months, and we shall discuss later the development of his own ideas on "Europe" during that period. When he resigned in January 1946 the prevailing sentiment in all French governmental circles, with the partial exception of the Socialists, was still, as I have said, that the Germans should be kept down and if possible made to pay for the war by the cession of the Saar, the formation of an autonomous Rhineland and, under four-power aegis perhaps, some special regime for the Ruhr. In short, Germany ought to be dismembered, France should more or less regain her "natural" frontiers and the various separate German states should somehow be kept in order by the four victorious powers.

This policy was vigorously pursued, notably by Bidault, but when it shortly became clear (in 1946–1947) that it was quite unacceptable to France's Western allies—who on 1 January 1947 actually united their respective occupation zones, over-ruling French objections—the emphasis came increasingly to be laid on the idea of "containing" an always potentially dangerous Germany by the construction of some "European" body into which she could be absorbed and which she could not therefore dominate. This general conception was also favoured by some Frenchmen who thought in terms broader than the simple interests of France, and who saw the formation of a "federal" Europe as a good thing in itself, as tending towards the suppression of that excessive nationalism which many believed to have been responsible for a series of disastrous wars. Some of those who thought this way were French but there were also distinguished men in the Low Countries and in Italy who, during the occupation, or transported to Germany, had had time to brood over these problems. A great many were Socialists, but they tended to put their European faith above party politics. They were the inheritors of a great tradition.

Ever since the Middle Ages the idea of European unity had fascinated intellectuals, politicians and rulers in our turbulent sub-continent. Attempts to unify Europe by force had been responsible for many major wars. If you exclude Russia, the three great traditional European nations of the mainland—namely Spain, France and (in various guises) Germany —had all made this attempt and all had been defeated by a coalition of which England had been the heart and soul. But equally all efforts to unite the Continent by consent had ended dismally. Apart from the "Holy Alliance" at the beginning of the 19th Century, such schemes, indeed, had hardly ever got off the drawing-board. The latest governmental scheme had been the ill-fated "Briand Plan" in the early thirties for a European Economic Union. The latest prophet, spiritual descendant of Sully, the Abbé St Pierre, Kant, Bentham, Victor Hugo and Proudhon, was Count Coudenhove-Kalergi,[1] founder of the Pan-European Movement. After the war which, after all had imposed a German "New Order" that worked for four years after a fashion, the most active organizer and, as it were, the high priest of the movement, was Jean Monnet, a brilliant brandy-merchant from the Charente, who had not joined General de Gaulle in London and had spent the early part of the war in America where he was largely responsible for the successful co-ordination of the Allied war effort (the "Combined Boards") and obtained the lifelong trust of many American and British politicians and officials. It is quite possible that this wave of organized enthusiasm for the Federal cause would have succeeded anyhow; but, as I say, it was powerfully assisted by the early and complete failure of the Council of Foreign Ministers to arrive at agreement on the German question and to the consequent necessity, from the point of view of France, of achieving security by other than purely diplomatic or forceful means which had failed so lamentably in the past, and never so lamentably as after World War I.

By the end of 1947, however, the "Cold War" had broken out in its full intensity. The Treaty of Dunkirk between France and Britain was signed in March of that year; but "War" was, as it were, officially declared by the "*Coup de Prague*" in March 1948, when the Communists seized power in Czechoslovakia. This was followed, almost immediately, by

[1] Now an enthusiastic advocate of de Gaulle's nationalistic theses.

the Berlin Blockade. It was therefore clear by early 1948 that some close military association of the Western Powers was essential if the Soviet Union was to be prevented from gaining—not necessarily by actual military occupation, but more probably by the establishment of Communist or pro-Communist governments—the upper hand in Western Europe. After this fact had been recognized by the then British Foreign Secretary, Mr Bevin, in his great speech of 22 January 1948, first the Brussels Treaty Organization, consisting of France, Britain and the Low Countries, came into being in the spring and negotiations were then set on foot for what became the North Atlantic Treaty, signed in April 1949 and ratified in the summer of that year.

Meanwhile, the effort to create "Europe" had continued. Powerfully stimulated by Winston Churchill's speech at Zürich in September 1946 in which he called for Franco-German reconciliation and urged "Europeans" to come together in face of the external threat to their liberties, the famous Conference of the Hague was convoked (7–10 May 1948) and the European Movement was born. Pressure on governments to take some action was irresistible and negotiations for what was to become the Council of Europe were begun in the autumn of 1948, the Statute being signed on 8 May 1949. It was at this point—as I well remember because I was one of the British negotiating team—that the European (and more particularly the French) Federalists suffered a major reverse. Already at the Hague Conference all the running had been made by the British Conservatives, then in opposition, the British Labour Party being scarcely represented. And when it came to official negotiations it was absolutely clear that the Labour Party was opposed to the whole Federal concept and was anyhow much more Atlantic than European-minded.

Engaged on a major programme of internal rehabilitation, they were busy nationalizing certain key industries and, as a bitter Socialist once remarked, there is nothing that Socialists nationalize so well as Socialism. In any case the nationalist sentiments of Messrs Attlee and Bevin were at that moment shared by a great majority of the British people. The very idea of actually joining up with the "Continentals," practically all of whom had been defeated while alone among the European nations Great Britain had preserved her integrity and her self-respect, was at that time inconceivable. "How," said Sir Stafford Cripps contemptuously to an eager American preaching some Anglo-French union, "How would you like it if we asked *you* to go to bed with Brazil?"

It was thus inevitable that the Council of Europe should have been founded, not on the federal, but rather on the opposite principle of complete national independence. Its Assembly can, indeed, pass resolutions, but they are normally unheeded by the Council of Ministers which has to proceed by way of unanimity. There is indeed no supra-national element whatever in the Statute, which there might have been even if the Federal thesis had been largely discarded. The same principle of unanimity was, naturally, applied to the other great European structure of this period, the Organization for European Economic Cooperation (OEEC), founded in April 1948, to distribute Marshall Aid, the United Kingdom assuming

the permanent chairmanship. Nothing, perhaps, typi-
fied the British attitude at that time towards "Europe"
better than this organization, the success of which
in eliminating obstacles to trade and in putting the
Western European States on their feet during approxi-
mately a ten-year period was undisputed.

Hence the United Kingdom, with her Commonwealth and Empire, was, as Churchill said in 1953,
"with" but not "of" Europe. She was also, in a way,
the link between "Europe" and the United States. It
was the famous policy of the "three overlapping
circles"—UK–USA, UK–Commonwealth, UK–
Europe—which, insofar as it ever had any real
validity, was no longer even theoretically tenable in
the late fifties when the Commonwealth gradually
faded out, when "Europe" was formed, and when
there was no longer any "special relationship" with
the USA. This general attitude, however, seemed to
be accepted by other Western European Governments
until 9 May 1950.

There then occurred an event of great importance.
For some time previously, and in secret talks with the
Germans, Jean Monnet, assisted by some of the most
brilliant young men of the period, had been preparing
a spectacular plan for the joint control of the coal and
steel industries of Western Europe. This project,
which became known as the European Coal and Steel
Community (ECSC), contained the highly original
and, indeed, revolutionary feature of a "communal"
Executive called the High Authority which consisted
of nine international civil servants. This Authority
could, by the requisite majority, actually take decisions binding on the six governments concerned,

which made it the first genuinely supra-national organization that had ever been created in Europe by consent rather than by force. For the other executive body, namely the Council of Ministers, though it would obviously have great influence, was only designed to be a sort of link between the Authority and the various governments. For its part, the Assembly, the parliamentary body composed of 78 members, was only given limited powers. But there was also a Court of Justice which had the right to interpret the Treaty and receive (not only from states but also from individuals and firms) appeals against the actions of the High Authority. It was, in other words, based on the principles which the French negotiators had unsuccessfully attempted to insert into the Statute of the Council of Europe.

The scheme had already been sold to Robert Schuman, at that time Foreign Minister of France, a Lorrainer who had served in the German Army during the First World War, and it was he who launched it out of the blue on 9 May 1950. Schuman's main objective was to achieve a true reconciliation between France and Germany and, by pooling two industries vital to any country's national defence, to make it physically impossible for France and Germany to wage war against each other. But it was also an invitation to Germany to participate as an equal partner in the construction of Europe. "Five years almost to the day after the unconditional surrender of Germany," Schuman said at his Press Conference, "France takes the first positive step towards European constructions and associates Germany with it."

The announcement was a great shock to the British

Labour Government. An attempt was made to sell the idea to Cripps, then Chancellor of the Exchequer, and to induce His Majesty's Government to take part in the ensuing negotiations, but only on condition that they agreed in advance to accept the principle of a European Authority which could, in the last resort, overrule national governments. Even if it had not contained a strong element of supra-nationalism, however, the British would probably not have been favourably disposed towards the project (though Britain had in fact been a member before the war of the European Iron and Steel Cartel). As it was, their opposition was inevitable, nor would the proposal in its supra-national form have met with the approval of the House of Commons.

A little later in the year, even Harold Macmillan— at that time in opposition—who on 17 August 1949 had circulated an amendment to the Statute of the Council of Europe that "the Committee of Ministers shall be an executive authority with supra-national powers: the Committee shall have its own permanent secretariat of European officials"—declared that we "could never allow any supra-national authority to close down our pits and steelworks." Anyhow, the Labour Government refused to take part in the negotiations for the drafting of the instrument, which was signed on 18 April 1951 between what have ever since become known as "the Six." It duly came into force on 25 July 1952. This was a real turning-point and the first major victory of the Federalists.

Very shortly after Robert Schuman's initiative, however, an even more earth-shaking event took place. On 25 June 1950 the North Koreans, with fairly obvious Russian approval and consent, invaded South Korea. Two days later the Security Council (in the absence of the Soviet representative) condemned the aggression and the U S A, armed with U N authority, rushed to the victims' support, being later joined by military forces from 15 allied countries. Many people thought that the Third World War was imminent. Had it not been for President Truman's action in dismissing General McArthur many held—some still hold—that it would in fact have broken out. It was therefore inevitable that tremendous efforts should have been made to strengthen the North Atlantic Treaty Organization (NATO) which had been gradually built up since 17 September 1949, when the North Atlantic Treaty effectively came into force. The old Brussels Treaty Military Headquarters at Fontainebleau was hastily absorbed into the new machine, General Eisenhower was appointed Supreme Commander in Europe (SACEUR) in December 1950, and the energies of the Western World were largely geared to producing at short notice a military apparatus at least comparable to the vast and menacing Soviet build-up on the Elbe. The fact that the United States still held a monopoly of the atomic bomb was almost forgotten in the process.

The assumed need for speed in rearmament and, so far as possible, for parity with the USSR, at any rate on land, had, however, one highly alarming consequence for France. Scarcely were the Americans in the saddle, directing the continued defensive effort of the new Alliance, than they came to the conclusion that defence was impossible unless the newly-united Western Germans were allowed to join NATO and

consequently to re-arm. In spite of, and perhaps because of, their complete dependence, both military and
economic, on the Americans during the first few post-
war years, the French had never been as enthusiastic
for NATO as the British. It was rather accepted as
a slightly disagreeable necessity. But the thought that,
within it, they would be expected to be no more important or significant than their ex-enemies was even
more disagreeable. Might it not even be that the
Germans would become the favoured ally of the
Americans and from that vantage point once again
dream of hegemony in Europe? Evidently, if Russian
domination was to be avoided, it would be difficult to
stand out against at all events *some* rearmament of
the Germans; but, if so, how were the very real
dangers inherent in such consent to be mitigated?

The answer was a scheme for an actual merger of
the armed forces of Germany and France through the
medium of a European Defence Community (EDC).
The original plan for a European Army had been
already mooted at the Hague Conference of 1948.
Here Churchill, without specifically saying so, seems
to have given the impression that the United Kingdom
would actually take part in the scheme, or at least
closely associate herself with it. Subsequently a very
detailed project for a European Army was worked
out by the able René Pleven, one of de Gaulle's supporters in London who subsequently joined a small
Centre party. The new force was to be "integrated"
right down to battalion level and elaborate arrangements were made for the formation of a single general
staff.

Later, in the Treaty itself, provision was made for

integration at divisional level only, but there was to
be not only a Council of Ministers and a special
Assembly, but also a Board of Commissioners with
significant powers in the field of arms procurement.
The whole machine, in other words, was the equivalent of a federal political structure based on the
principle of the separation of powers and a bicameral
system of representation. During the debates on it in
the Council of Europe at Strasbourg late in 1950
Churchill had even voted for an amendment of Paul
Reynaud's that "it [the Army] shall operate under
the authority of a single European Minister of
Defence." The Treaty was signed in the spring of
1951 and its ratification by the French Parliament was
confidently expected.

Towards the end of that year, however, the British
Tories turned out the Labour Government and came
back into power with a workable majority. All the
"Europeans" expected that, after what Churchill and
his colleagues had said while they were in opposition
about the necessity of founding Europe in a serious
sense, there was great hope for progress here. In particular, they expected some statement which would
at least assist the ratification of the European Defence
Community on which lay the hopes of democratic
France for a long-term solution of the German problem.

It was therefore with dismay that, after a rather
guarded declaration at Strasbourg by David Maxwell-
Fyfe, the "Europeans" learned that the new Foreign
Secretary, Anthony Eden, in a speech at Rome, had
made it clear that the British Government would
have absolutely nothing to do with the project. It has

been alleged that Eden had received American advice counselling him against encouraging the European Army project on the grounds that it would take a long time to run in and that the great thing was to get on with arming the Germans speedily. Whatever the reasons, the attitude of the Tory Government undoubtedly reinforced the suspicion with which Great Britain is normally regarded on the other side of the Channel and Paul-Henri Spaak resigned from the Presidency of the Assembly of the Council of Ministers. Nevertheless the French Government proceeded with the scheme, though it did not yet feel strong enough to put it to the test of ratification.[2]

During 1952 and 1953 France was reorganizing her economy and was more and more involved in the war against the Vietnamese Communists, for which, however, the Americans largely paid in arms and credits. NATO was being formed, though the initial impetus had partly run out. The OEEC was still functioning well. The Fourth Republic, though Government succeeded Government with a rather startling rapidity, provided an excellent administration. The EDC, though increasingly attacked, still seemed to many to offer the right solution for the all-important German problem. The Communist Party, associated with the horrors of the Stalinist regime in Russia, was largely discredited and became known as "the stranded whale." The Gaullists, after their initial electoral successes, were breaking up and becoming absorbed in the "system." On the whole, the country seemed

[2] Many great authorities, including Jacques Fauvet and Guy de Carmoy believe however that they could have got it through if they had really tried.

to be settling down. Two things disturbed this quite satisfactory course of events. In the first place, the conflict in far-away Indo-China was slowly going from bad to worse. In the second place, the death of Stalin on 6 March 1953 seemed to throw open to question some of the assumptions on which the foreign policy of a more or less united West had rested since the "*Coup de Prague.*"

The year 1954 also witnessed two events of great significance. In the spring and summer there was a conference at Geneva on Viet Nam which resulted in a settlement based on the (assumed temporary) division of the country. This settlement was a great triumph for Anthony Eden, whose negotiating talents were never seen to better advantage. It was also a triumph for the new French Prime Minister, Pierre Mendès-France, who had clearly, if unconsciously, been nominated by the French nation to clear up an impossible situation. It was finally remarkable for the emergence on the international scene of a rather new kind of Soviet representative who was at least prepared to talk in a reasonably practical way with his Western opposite number. Since at the end of the conference the British Foreign Secretary and his Russian opposite number, Mr Molotov, were designated as continuing "co-chairmen" it was clear that, to some extent, the Russians were emerging from a period of almost total isolation and were preparing to assume a slightly more co-operative role in international affairs.

The second event was the rejection in the late summer by the French Parliament of the European Defence Community. As the extreme tension in East-

West relations gradually diminished, so the opposition in France of nationalists and communists to the complicated and supra-national features of the EDC increased in volume and in influence. This opposition eventually spread to the French Socialist Party, some prominent members of which had always been resolutely opposed to the idea. So, when the new forceful French Premier, after solving the Vietnamese problem at Geneva, felt himself strong enough at least to put the question directly to the National Assembly on 30 August, it was not approved and the entire project collapsed. It was true that the Premier had not pressed the point unduly, and had indeed told members of his own Government, some of whom were Gaullists, that they could vote as their consciences dictated. This was because he himself had genuine doubts about the practicability of the scheme and even greater doubts about his own ability to obtain a majority for it in the Assembly. In the light of hindsight it looks as if his judgment was correct. The French were no longer as frightened of the Russians as they had been. The project was almost certainly doomed.

Its rejection was, however, a major blow, not only to the general policy of building up the Atlantic Alliance with a German military contribution, but also to the basic French intention of somehow coming to terms with the Germans in a supra-national association of some kind so as, once and for all, to avoid yet another German attempt to dominate the Continent. The first set-back resulted in feverish diplomatic activity. The British Foreign Secretary toured Europe in an effort to find some alternative solution to the problem of German rearmament. Eventually he presided over a conference in London at which, with considerable difficulty,[3] he was persuaded to pledge the country not to reduce the existing British ground and air forces in Germany except with the consent of a majority in the Council of Ministers. It is true that this concession was hedged about with "let-out" clauses, one relating to the right of the United Kingdom to draw on these forces if needed to meet some overseas emergency of a colonial nature, and another to a right of appeal to the Council of Ministers if a reduction should seem to be essential for balance-of-payments reasons. But the concessions made were sufficient to enable Mendès-France eventually to get the whole scheme for a "Western European Union" through the French Parliament, though it was rejected once before the Treaty of Paris, signed on 23 October 1954, was finally ratified by the French Assembly on 30 December.

In making his gesture towards supra-nationalism as regards the British forces in Germany, Anthony Eden no doubt thought that he had in some way mitigated the painful effect in France of his complete rejection, some three years previously, of any idea of British association with the EDC. Possibly he also thought that the gesture which saved the conference had also settled the future role of France in Europe. If he did, he was mistaken. It is true that at the beginning of 1955 the hopes of the "Federalists" had almost touched rock-bottom. The "unanimity" thesis of the "Anglo-Saxons," to say nothing of the French nationalists, seemed to have finally prevailed. The Coal and

[3] Anthony Nutting, *Europe Will Not Wait*, p. 74.

Steel Community could not, by itself, result in any great measure of "European" unity. Unless it was somehow reinforced, it also might eventually collapse. Already schemes for some kind of Industrial Free Trade Area, not necessarily confined to Europe, were being mooted in the OEEC. Once again recourse was had to the ever ingenious, devoted and resourceful Jean Monnet. The situation was all the graver because just after the French Assembly had rejected the plan for a European Defence Community the Algerian rebellion, which was destined to hold down most of the French Army for nearly eight years, had broken out in the distant mountains of the Aurès.

Monnet wasted no time. Once again he collected a brilliant and devoted team. There was a meeting at Bergen in Norway which was much influenced by Jan Beyen of the Netherlands and then, in May, he induced the French Government (Edgar Faure now being Foreign Minister) to organize a conference which met in June 1956 at Messina. The subject for discussion was nothing less than the establishment, not of a Free Trade Area, but of a full-blown European Customs Union. Everyone knew where Customs Unions had led in the past. There was the example of the Prussian Zollverein of 1818 which played a large part in the establishment of the Second German Empire. Indeed behind the project for a Customs Union lay the idea of an Economic Union, and conscious thought was even then devoted to this wider project.

The British were asked to send a high-level representative to the Messina Conference of Foreign Ministers, but they contented themselves with sending an observer from the Board of Trade, who was present also when in the autumn the negotiations were transferred to Brussels but was soon withdrawn. Frankly, the conviction of the British Government at that time was that these negotiations could not possibly succeed; and even if they did, Britain did not want to be associated with anything like a Customs, still less with an Economic Union. In November 1956, when the negotiations, now *à six*, were entering their final phase, Harold Macmillan, Chancellor of the Exchequer, and soon to be Prime Minister, said: "So this [Commonwealth] objection, even if no other, would be quite fatal to any proposal that the United Kingdom should seek to take part in a European Common Market by going into a Customs Union."

No doubt the declarations of statesmen, like treaties, can only have a limited validity in time, in this case about four years. *Tempora mutantur nos et mutamur in illis.* But what is certain is that in 1955–56 the British Government, and British public opinion generally, would not have agreed to go much further than contemplate entry into some kind of Free Trade Area with perhaps, as in the Western European Union, some faint element of supra-nationalism. This does not mean that the Government was right not to insist on a continued British presence during the negotiations. At the least they might have influenced the provisions for the entry of new members! Anyhow, the Treaty of Rome was duly signed on 25 March 1957, and ratified on 9 July of that year. It was the end of an epoch.

Meanwhile the Algerian War continued and the Fourth Republic was finding it increasingly difficult to assert its authority over the Algerian *colons*. Suddenly, in July 1956, President Nasser nationalized the Suez Canal and in the ensuing feverish period of diplomatic activity the French leaders saw a great light. If they were able, by physical force if need be, to topple Nasser, then the spirit would go out of the Algerian nationalist movement which he was actively supporting, and the *"Loi Cadre"* providing for Algerian autonomy within the French Union could be successfully imposed. The only visible means of toppling Nasser, short of direct military intervention by France and Britain, which seemed almost impossible in the prevailing international climate, was by fixing up some arrangement with the Government of Israel and drawing the British into it. Then, after the victory and the pacification of Algeria, which would powerfully reinforce the position of France, the moment might arrive at which the British could come nearer to "Europe" and a system be elaborated in which what we have defined as the basic objective of France could be achieved, namely control of Germany through common institutions.

As everybody now knows, the scheme miscarried. The French forces had indeed distinguished themselves—some might hold that they had even been more effective than the British. Certainly the French paratroopers had had more experience of battle conditions than their British allies. But, politically, Suez ended in something near national humiliation, though admittedly in much more humiliation for Britain than for France. In any case, what small opposition there might have been in France to the conclusion of a Common Market without the United Kingdom, resting as it did essentially on intimate Franco-German co-operation, largely vanished. Though it may to some extent have been a coincidence, there is no doubt that the Treaty of Rome was signed only four months after the withdrawal from the Suez area of Franco-British forces. General de Gaulle is said later to have observed that "You have to be called Guy Mollet or Pineau to believe in the military virtues of the English."[4] Anyhow, as a result of the Suez disaster, as Dorothy Pickles says in her in many ways excellent book,[5] France was indeed beginning "to learn to live with Germany and like it, and without Great Britain without minding it." What was clear was that by mid-1957 France and Britain were going separate ways. Realizing this, the British Government made desperate efforts to secure the general adoption of the principles of a general Industrial Free Trade Area. Reginald Maudling was appointed the chief salesman of this doomed conception. In spite of his efforts the EEC came into force on 1 January 1958, and it was pretty clear, even then, what this would lead to.

After Suez had been cleared up there was also much more talk of a "detente" in East-West relations. The solution of the Viet Nam issue in negotiations with the Russians had encouraged such hopes. A "Summit" meeting had already been held at Geneva in July 1955 and a meeting of Foreign Ministers in the following November. But these were the days before the dynamic Nikita Khrushchev had stepped up tension over Berlin. In May 1958 it looked as if the so-called

[4] Tournoux, *La Tragédie du Géneral*, Plon, 1967, p. 214.
[5] *The Uneasy Entente*, Chatham House Essays, 1967, p. 32.

"Balance of Terror" was making any major war more and more improbable. China had not yet broken officially with Russia. The "Third World" had not yet, as it were, reached boiling point. The West had successfully consolidated its forces under the aegis of America. To sum up, the situation at the moment when a "Gaullist" European policy, the subject of this essay, may be deemed to have come into being was as follows.

France was a fairly contented partner in a nine-year-old Atlantic Alliance, but the initial willing acceptance of American leadership in this alliance was wearing off. Nevertheless such leadership was still regarded as essential for French security, at any rate for the duration of the Algerian war. France had, however, decided that, provided she could get German agreement to an agricultural deal in return for French acceptance of German industrial competition, she would join up with Western Germany in what was officially destined to become a European Economic Union which the British had always strongly opposed and which they showed no signs of accepting, still less of joining. This Community had not yet come into active operation and it was open to the French, if they so desired, to hold up its operation almost indefinitely. The main point was, however, that the French had already broken with a British-led non-supra-national Europe and had, in principle, preferred to this a supra-national Europe with Germany as the principal partner.

In spite of the success of The Queen's visit to Paris in the spring of 1957 (arranged before Suez), the "Entente Cordiale" had to all intents and purposes disappeared, and a period of rather strained relations with the United Kingdom had already begun. The process of "retreat from Empire" had started in Indo-China, had already spread to Tunisia and Morocco, and looked as if it might be continued in Algeria too. It had given rise to a good deal of anti-American, if not anti-"Anglo-Saxon" feeling. In any case a new deal of some kind was obviously impending for the whole of the overseas "French Community." At the beginning of 1958 the young, penultimate Prime Minister of the Fourth Republic, Félix Gaillard, had authorized the construction of an atomic bomb. Such was the state of France when a military revolt in Algiers resulted in the arrival in power of the "providential man."

2

De Gaulle's Plan for "Europe" Up Till 1958

ALL HIS LIFE, says de Gaulle in his memoirs, he has had "a certain idea" of France, and there is no doubt that, all his life, he has been constant in his adoration of "France," which he sees as "a Madonna in a fresco." But has he, all his life, had a "certain idea" of Europe? The answer is, No. Until he was well over 50, de Gaulle does not seem to have had any ideas about "Europe" except as a geographical expression. Larousse says that "Europe" is "the smallest, but the most heavily populated, part of the world, contained within the Arctic Ocean on the North, the Atlantic Ocean on the West, the Mediterranean and its annexes and the Caucasus on the South, the Ural mountains and the Ural river on the East." This he certainly never forgot.

Before examining de Gaulle's European policy from 1958–68, and its effects—which is the main object of this book—we may, therefore, profitably take a look at his expressed views (a) during the period when he was in charge of "La France Combattante," in London and Algiers, and subsequently, for eighteen months, in charge of France herself, that is to say, from 1940 to early 1946, and (b) during his "period in the wilderness," that is to say, from February 1946 until May 1958. In doing so we can perhaps assume that he was rather more careful in the expression of his views during the first period than during the second, when his utterances sometimes seemed to have more the quality of meditation or sombre prophecy.

Apart from (rather reluctantly) under-writing the abortive proposal for an actual Franco-British Union in June 1940; declaring, at Oxford on 25 November

1941, that after the War, France and Britain would have to achieve "collaboration of a new type"; and predicting, in his Albert Hall speech of 11 November 1942, the emergence of a "tortured Europe from the Pyrenees to the Volga," de Gaulle waited until he came into effective power in Algeria during 1943 to produce anything like a coherent European thesis. This was after long consultations with his supporters and notably with representatives of the French Resistance, most of whom, as we saw in the last chapter, were enthusiastic Europeans, and, indeed, for the most part Federalists. After consultation, too, with people like René Mayer, who had had important business connections with Germany before the war, and with other members of the Committee of National Liberation. With his approval René Massigli had already prepared a report on a "new Europe" which would emerge from the Resistance. This contemplated "the association of the Rhineland with a Western Bloc," and an actual "Federation between France, Belgium, Luxembourg and Holland, which Great Britain might join also." All this preparatory work culminated in the speech of 18 May 1944 before the Assembly in Algiers.

The main features of the scheme sketched out in this speech were that, once the cancer of "Prussian Germanism" had been removed, France could "assume a European role for the benefit of everybody." But there would have to be a certain "balance" and France was therefore thinking in terms of a "kind of Western grouping," chiefly economic, and as widely based as possible, which might be constructed on French initiative (*réalisé avec nous*). Such a grouping could have an African prolongation and would be in close touch with the Arab States. The Channel, the Rhine and the Mediterranean would be, as it were, its arteries, and it might form an indispensable nucleus (*un centre capital*) in "a World Organization for production, exchanges and security." It will be observed that, on the face of it, this "grouping," of which France would be the natural centre, would include not only the United Kingdom but, potentially, Germany, the Low Countries, Italy, the Iberian Peninsula and, conceivably, Yugoslavia and Greece as well.

According to Edmond Jouve,[1] the General at this point confessed to one of his Commissioners that he did indeed contemplate a "Europe" which could include Italy, Spain and Portugal, "as soon as they returned to democracy," and Switzerland too if she wanted to join. Germany also should certainly join but only, of course, if she was dismembered and dispossessed of her "formidable arsenal." The Ruhr would then produce and deliver the goods necessary for the "grouping," and the Rhineland should be the "common property" of the new Europe. France would, in any case, play an essential role. She was the "most numerous" and the "most powerful,"[2] and could thus constitute the corner-stone (*assise*) of the whole

[1] "Le General de Gaulle et la construction de l'Europe" (Lib. Gen. de Droit et de Jurisprudence) Vol. I, p. 10.

[2] Something must have gone wrong here, or the General was 120 years out of date. The UK, Italy and Western Germany each have considerably more inhabitants than France, whose gross national product is also much lower than that of Western Germany.

new organization. No specific mention seems to have been made of the United Kingdom! It will be seen that in this original formulation of Gaullist thought on Europe considerable emphasis was laid on the idea of some very close association of nations in Western Europe and even on a "Federation." This last idea was to be taken up again nearly ten years later and we will discuss it in the second part of this Chapter after we have concluded our examination of the General's thought on Europe while he was in power for the first time. But now we must have recourse to the *Mémoires*.

On page 47 *et seq.* of the remarkable Third Volume[3] (written mostly, it is true, towards the end of the period of exile and consequently some ten years after the event) de Gaulle describes his thoughts in the autumn of 1944. After outlining his own well-known plan for the dismemberment of Germany, shared, as we have already seen, by most Frenchmen at that moment, the General says that all this would fit in very well with "my own idea of Europe." Europe, he goes on, could only find a "balance" by "an association between Slavs, Germans, Gauls and Latins." No doubt "Bolshevism"—and it will be remembered that these thoughts are supposed to have been formulated before Soviet troops had set foot in Poland—would endeavour to impose its rule in the regions of the Vistula, the Danube and the Balkans. "But as soon as Germany was no longer a menace, such subordination, no longer justified, would sooner or later become intolerable for the vassals, and the Russians themselves would lose all desire to stray beyond their own

[3] *Le Salut 1944–46*, Plon, 1959.

frontiers." Even if the Kremlin insisted on dominating
these countries it would finally be unable to resist
national wills and, in any case, if the Western Allies
intervened with the Soviet Government "in a firm and
united way" the independence of the Poles, Czechs,
Hungarians and the Balkan peoples could doubtless be
assured. "This having been done, the unity of Europe
could be gradually constructed in the form of an
organized association of its peoples from Iceland to
Istanbul and from Gibraltar to the Urals."

De Gaulle says that he knew very well that this
plan might never be applied but that he was convinced
"that France could take effective action in this sense;
play a splendid role; and greatly further her own
interests and those of the human race." But first it was
necessary to put an end to French exclusion from the
discussions that were proceeding on the subject. There
was some chance of putting it across since "nothing
which they (the Three) had decided about Europe . . .
could be applied without French consent. France
would shortly be on the Rhine with a respectable
army and at the end of the war would be in a position
of authority (*debout*) in the old Continent while
America would find herself back in her hemisphere
and Britain in her island." Provided the will was there,
therefore, France would be able to "break the circle
of resigned acceptance and tame renunciation in
which our partners wanted to confine us."

With all this in mind, he invited Churchill and
Eden to Paris and they arrived on 10 November 1944.
After much public display and many affecting ceremonies they got down to business. France, de Gaulle
declared, was being reborn, but it was evident that it

would be a little while before she recovered her old
strength. The British, for their part, would come out
of the war covered with glory, but, unjust though
this might be, their relative position might well be
diminished, given the losses and wastages of the war,
the centrifugal forces in the Commonwealth, and,
above all, the rise of America and Russia, and even of
China. Since, therefore, Britain and France would
both be seriously weakened, why should they not
combine their strength? If, more especially, *they
could agree to act in common on all outstanding issues
they could ensure that nothing would be done which
they could not jointly accept.* (My italics.) This concept could be the basis for a real alliance. By this
means, too, "an Organization of Nations" might be
formed in Europe which could otherwise become a
simple object of dispute between America and Russia.
In other words, acting together, "Britain and France
could work for peace just as, twice in thirty years,
they had together faced a war." According to the
General, the appeal fell on deaf ears. Churchill thought
that all he could do was to try to influence the Super-
Powers. He was not prepared directly to confront
them—or at least America. It was agreed that France
should join the European Commission in London, but
that was all.

De Gaulle decided to go at once to Moscow. Before
going, he described his general policy in a speech to
the National Assembly on 22 November 1944. France
should possess "the elementary security which nature
had placed on the banks of the Rhine," as should the
Low Countries and, to a large extent, Britain as well
and such a settlement would allow "the fruitful con-

struction of European unity." "We believe in that," de Gaulle proclaimed, "and we hope that, to begin with, it will take the form of precise agreements binding the three poles, Moscow, London and Paris." It was thus after introducing Russia, for the first time, into his European conception that he hurried off to discover whether at any rate Stalin would be favourably disposed towards his general policy.

At his first meeting with the Ruler of all the Russias on 2 December, de Gaulle, rebuffed by Churchill, had no hesitation in putting forward a similar plan to a different partner. He suggested "*a direct understanding between the Governments of Moscow and Paris in order to fix the basis of a settlement which they would propose in common to the other allies.*" (My italics.) But Stalin was no better disposed to this idea than Churchill, and, indeed, for much the same reasons. What had de Gaulle to offer? He had to be content with a treaty similar to the existing Anglo-Russian one. An idea which, I seem to remember, originated with myself, and was approved by the Foreign Secretary, that there should be a tripartite treaty, was indignantly rejected.

Nothing separated France and Russia politically, de Gaulle explained to Stalin, but with Britain there were a number of differences which would have to be resolved before any treaty could be signed. There was, therefore, nothing much to report to the National Assembly on his return, except to explain the workings and significance of the Franco-Soviet Pact and why it was not at present possible to have a similar pact with Britain or America. France was, of course, not invited to the Yalta Conference (February 1945) and it was no doubt this fact, much more than what was actually agreed there, that gave rise to the subsequent legend that the Anglo-Saxons had handed over half Europe to the Russians at the Conference with hardly a protest.

Later in the year, however (22 September 1945), de Gaulle described *Western* Europe, including Germany and, in principle, Iberia, as a "natural complex"—geographical, economic and cultural—which, taken as a whole, was capable of forming an "ensemble" not inferior to other "economic masses" in the modern world. In this area France and Britain were the two principal powers whose task was "to guide the other nations towards a greater material development, a greater political maturity and a higher level of civilization." If either of them "lost her possessions" the other would also "become an anomaly" and would in turn be dislodged from its position. They must therefore work together and it was "an absurdity" for Britain to take part in decisions about the future of Germany without France.

But it was time for the General to bring to an end his first effort to re-establish France in her own eyes and in those of foreigners, believing that, before long, he would be recalled by the French people who had turned against the "system" which, as he saw it, could not possibly work. At that moment, too, the world situation might well have developed to a point more favourable to the application of his own ideas, which clearly at the moment were unacceptable not only to the French but also to the Allies. Before leaving, he delivered a valedictory speech which expressed both his bitterness and his hope. "We intend," he told the National Assembly on 10 December 1945, "to maintain friendly relations with the East and the West with our eyes open and our hands free. Such a policy may indeed result, for the time being, in the two very great Powers exceptionally agreeing to keep France at arm's length. We regret such *contretemps* for them, for us and for the world. But we know that our balance coincides with the balance of peace and we are quite determined not to abandon it, certain, as we are that, after various oscillations, it will finally be on our attitude that, to the advantage of all, the needle of the scale will finally rest." It looked as if a dispirited General had for the time being given up a then rather unequal struggle.

In 1946, indeed, the mind of General de Gaulle was on other things. He was preparing the ground for his *Rassemblement du Peuple Français* which, as he saw it, was destined to sweep away the hated "system" of parties and bring in a Constitution in line with his own ideas propounded at Bayeux on 18 June 1946. He was increasingly preoccupied, too, with the Russian attitude which was evidently dividing "Europe" into two hostile camps. In a speech at Bar-le-Duc on 28 July he deplored this development and the consequent increasing difficulty of reaching any agreement on Germany, who nevertheless must never again be "tempted" to indulge her old passion for conquest. How, then, could a "balance" be established (the notion of "balance" comes henceforward more and more into his utterances), and how could "old Europe," once "the guide of the universe," become again "the heart of the world"? He thinks it can if "the nations of the ancient West whose vital arteries are" (as before) "the North Sea, the Mediterranean and the Rhine" could "concert their policies." And "such a harmony would imply first of all an understanding between London and Paris."

There is little change in his European outlook in 1947, nor in the first half of 1948. The "balance" must somehow be preserved. There must (Paris, 9 July 1947) be a "real agreement" between Britain and France. The Germans must still be divided up into "states," or perhaps a federation of states (Paris Press Conference 12 November). The idea of a definite agreement with the United Kingdom is repeated at this Press Conference when the need for a common defence of the West is also recognized. At Marseilles (17 April 1948) the General even admits that his original idea of co-operating with Russia was "an illusion." Only when it had been possible to "construct a Western Europe of which the physical and moral centre would be France" would it also be possible to establish a real peace with the USSR. But on 9 June 1948 (in Paris) we reach a turning point. It is occasioned by the "London Communiqué" of the three Western Allies on Germany. French objections have been largely overcome and a Western German Federal Government may shortly emerge. It thus becomes impossible to think in terms of German "states." How could they, in any case, have been formed, given the necessity of preparing for what seemed to be the imminent danger of invasion from the East? At the end of 1948 it was clear that the whole basis of French foreign policy as conducted since 1945 was crumbling and that all French leaders would shortly have to discover some new political philosophy. De

Gaulle was one of the first to do so, though not at once.

In his vehement denunciation of the "London Communiqué" we do hear indeed the first overt note of suspicion as regards the United Kingdom who may, it seems, "be trying to arrange for a renaissance of the Reich so that, in any Western European grouping, France and Germany may become of equal weight and thus allow Britain to act as an umpire." Nor from now on, do we hear for some time of any "grouping" which explicitly includes the United Kingdom. England becomes "an island" (1 October, Paris). Europe cannot be defended from London (1 December, Paris). And on 12 February 1949 (in Lille), though all hope for German "States" has not been abandoned, France herself "must be at the head of any 'European' organization," failing which "the enterprise will have no head and the organization no centre." The same note prevails in a passionate address to the RPF in April.

By 25 September 1949 (when the General spoke at Bordeaux) the North Atlantic Treaty had been ratified, after vigorous debates in the French National Assembly. It had not been opposed by the General himself, who, indeed, at that time recognized that massive American military aid was essential if the menace of Soviet aggression was to be avoided. (At one stage de Gaulle believed that the Russians might arrive in Paris and that he himself might have to withdraw to Canada!)[4] The German Federal Republic had actually been proclaimed. The defence of the West could thus no longer be contemplated by anybody on

[4] Tournoux, op. cit., p. 54.

the basis of some Franco-British alliance, with France in the lead, France in virtual command of an "autonomous" Rhineland, and the other German "States" in friendly, if slightly subordinate, relations with Western Europe. So at Bordeaux, some seven months before Robert Schuman, as we have already noted, made his own spectacular move in the German direction, de Gaulle drew his own conclusions. "The man of good sense," he said, "would recognize that the Germans are where they are, that is to say in the middle of the Continent, and as they are, that is to say numerous, disciplined and dynamic, economically powerful, and once they have ceased to be led astray by the rage of conquest, capable of attaining the highest levels in science and in the arts."

He sees also Europe deprived, by Soviet domination, of a large and precious part of herself. England, he finds, is sailing off [s'éloigne] attracted by the transatlantic land-mass. He concludes that a United Europe must, if possible, and in spite of everything, include the Germans. But reason demands that, for this purpose, it must one day be possible to establish a direct and practical understanding between the German people and the French people reflecting the fact that they are in many respects complementary, and overcoming the vicissitudes of History. This, after all, is the heart of the problem. There will, or there will not, be a Europe depending on the possibility, or the impossibility, of arriving at a direct agreement between the Germans and the Gauls.

The new conception was pondered over at Colombey-les-deux-Eglises. The newly-formed Council of Europe was considered and (quite rightly) rejected as a real basis for European unity. It could not talk about any really important subjects and anyhow one member (Britain) had just devalued its currency without the slightest consultation with its European partners. On 14 November he alleged that he had "always" (which was not true) maintained that the "Europe" which he sought should be based on a direct agreement between the French and German peoples. He had imagined this taking place after a German "Confederation" had been established. Now, owing to the shortsighted policy of the Allies, it was necessary to contemplate a new Reich. So it was with the latter that any agreement should be signed.

Meanwhile his supporters had been by no means inactive. The fertile and ingenious Michel Debré, who had been a passionate "Atlanticist" and who by 1948 had become an even more passionate "European," came out in December 1949 with a draft "Fundamental Pact between the European States" of which the main feature was an "Arbiter" elected by a universal suffrage who, with Ministers from each member country, would be responsible for co-ordinating foreign policy. There was no mention of the Atlantic Alliance.

A year later plans for European Union were likewise submitted to the National Assembly by two devoted Gaullists, Gaston Palewski and General Billotte. The first plan would, after a preliminary referendum, establish a Confederation "within the Atlantic system," members preserving their sovereignty except insofar as they might give the Community powers concerning (among other things) defence, production and currency—which, on the face of it, seems pretty extensive. The second was more a counter-project to the much-detested European Army to be formed under the projected European Defence Community which would "clearly never be accepted by the United Kingdom." General Billotte also remarked, very intelligently, that "to try to create such a (supra-national) body without Britain, would tend to separate from the Anglo-Saxon world, and hence to bring into conflict with the Atlantic Union, the only Community disposing of indispensable strategic resources and the only one in which France and a confederated Europe might avoid a recrudescence of German tendencies towards an hegemony. In effect, the project would mean leaving France and Europe open to all the manoeuvres of Russian imperialism or German neo-Nazism or both combined." "Non-national" institutions were condemned, but a "Confederation," which would also cover defence, should be established, and Germany should be included in it subject to certain servitudes which should be defined by Treaty. Again, it was not clear exactly how decisions affecting foreign affairs and defence would be taken in such a "Confederation."

However, in a new draft submitted a year later (6 January 1953) by Michel Debré, the "Arbiter" disappears and is replaced by a "Political Council of Europe" which can actually "decide on the common policy to be followed by the signatory states in certain very large spheres including foreign policy and defence, such decisions being taken by a simple majority vote"! In other words the system was obviously supra-national in character and the "Europeans" of 1969 can only hope that the author, insofar as he may be responsible for the policy of France, will once again find some merit in his earlier convictions. There is no evidence, however, that any of these schemes had the direct approval of General de Gaulle, who, on 16 March 1950—still some two months ahead of Schuman's initiative—took up a suggestion just made by the new Chancellor, Adenauer, for an entente and perhaps one day a union between the two peoples.

Now he nailed his colours to a mast. He had, he said, often heard in the remarks of this "good German" an echo of the desperate voice of a ruined Europe calling on her children to unite. "After all, why should not the Rhine one day become a highway along which Europeans would meet each other, and no longer a ditch on the banks of which they always fought?" No victory had ever equalled that of the Catalaunian Fields where "the Franks, the Gauls, the Germans, and even the Romans, threw back Attila." What could not German and French valour, prolonged by Africa, if combined, achieve? In a word, it would be possible to resuscitate, in modern terms . . . "the whole conception of Charlemagne."

There was little doubt who the modern Charlemagne was likely to be, even though he would not in all probability install himself at Aix-la-Chapelle. What was certain was that from now on de Gaulle saw in Franco-German unity the essential and prerequisite basis for any possible European construction. Europe, which it was, of course, still very desirable to form, would gradually coalesce round this close association, the centre of which could only be Paris. This was something very different from the official policy of the Fourth Republic which, as we have seen, also chose Germany as the essential partner, but with the declared object of creating a supra-national Community, including Britain, of which both countries would be an integral part. The difference was indeed fundamental.

The fateful year 1950 proceeded and the North Korean War broke out. On that very day (25 June) in Paris de Gaulle further defined his thought. The Council of Europe was not "legitimate," and the unity of Europe therefore must spring from "an act of sovereignty" on the part of all its inhabitants. Nor was Schuman's new Coal and Steel Plan any good, because it depended on "unsubstantial" Public Authorities. There should thus be a "solemn referendum" among all "free" Europeans which should give rise to a "Federation," the main lines of which should be indicated. This "act of sovereignty" should nevertheless be coincidental, it would appear, with a direct agreement between France and Germany which would remain the essential basis of the whole affair. Besides, a France which had recovered her strength could only agree to her own Ministers and Generals being responsible for her own defence, which should be entirely autonomous in all spheres. The new "Federation" could not consequently be acceptable to France if it "dispersed French forces in a non-national (apatride) machine."

It was hence rather difficult to see how the intended new instrument could be a "Federation" in the normally accepted meaning of the word. The ambiguity persisted as the General elaborated on his new theme throughout the remainder of the year. In August, under the impact of the Korean War and its possible extension to Europe he was even talking of European institutions proceeding from a direct vote of the citizens of Europe which would dispose, in the spheres of the economy and of defence, of a portion of the sovereignty accorded to them by the participant states. But, here again, the proposal was immediately followed by a statement that, so far as defence was concerned, it would be for France to draw up a plan and to appoint a Commander-in-Chief, just as America would be expected to take the lead in Asia and Britain in the Middle East, the whole conception being crowned by a Council of the Three Powers with a combined General Staff. Under such a plan hope would be reborn from "the Atlantic to the Urals"—a phrase we shall hear much of as we go along.

The theme here propounded was continued in 1951, though at the beginning of that year de Gaulle was greatly concerned lest America should *not* defend Europe. A "massive" American force should be provided, though it was true that this should not be allowed to enable the Europeans to forgo their responsibilities, nor should it affect in any way their essential independence. In no case should the Americans conclude that they could defend Europe only by air and sea. The idea of a "non-national European Army" again came under heavy fire and was denounced as a "military Babel." A little later it became a "hybrid creation." Either it was the end of the French Army or it was bogus (*une fumisterie*). In June there is further reference to a Federation and, for the first time, the General admits that Germany must, to some degree, be responsible for her own defence. In September, European Unity is considered to be "still a myth"; but "the Atlantic Alliance, as it is applied, suppresses our independence without really protecting us."

On 4 November at St Mandé there is a further slight change: the "Federation" becomes a "Confederation," but it is evident that, as the General sees it, there is no distinction between the two terms, since on 25 November 1951, at a formal Press Conference in Paris, it is again a question of a body with a common "confederal" power to which each member remits a part of its own sovereignty, more especially as regards economics, defence and culture. There is a further attack on the Council of Europe and the ECSC, described as "unfortunate projects which can injure Europe" and, for the first time, it is the supranational element in the latter which is especially singled out for attack. The power concerned should rather be "confederal." Another important passage in this declaration ran as follows: "Great Britain, by reason of her insular situation, of her Commonwealth, of her traditions, is quite disinclined to incorporate herself in our Continent." Churchill had told him so, and Churchill's word must certainly be accepted.

During the whole of 1952 and 1953 he continued his intensive campaign in favour of his vague "Confederation" and a "direct agreement" between France and Germany. Increasingly it was represented as a rival project to the hated EDC and the "European Army." In speech after speech there are only minor variations on the general theme. Then, on 6 June 1952 in Paris, he solemnly "warns" the country that the latest decisions on the Army and on Germany were "*protocols d'abandon*" which would result in the disappearance of France: and on 8 October, in Paris, he observes that France, under the new "Atlantic" system, has already become a "protected state" and a mere "executant of other people's plans." As for the almost equally distasteful Coal and Steel Community it was an "imbroglio of pools" and (new thought) might well result in a *German* hegemony over Europe.

On 25 February, in Paris, it is the Council of Europe which is again under the lash. It has no "elementary or popular *élan*": nobody could possibly die for it. As for the EDC, the "Commissariat" which it would establish would be non-national (*apatride*) and could not, therefore, function; its "Assembly" would be bogus; and as for the Council of Ministers it would have to take its decisions by unanimous vote, which naturally meant that it could never take any decisions! (We ought, perhaps, to recall this apparent *lapsus* when we investigate the General's subsequent attitude towards a mild and limited form of weighted voting in the EEC.) Europe, indeed, could only be organized on a basis of nations. There could be no "fusion," only "association," which could most probably take the form of an "alliance." The alliance (again a new thought) might best be run by a Council of Heads of Government with a Commissariat, though of course not one with any "sovereign" powers. Every member should engage itself to defend every other member. The UK might agree to come into such an alliance and would play a great role if she did so. On the basis of this Alliance the well-known Conferedation would be founded after a previous Referendum. It was not then (June 1953) absolutely clear whether Britain would be a member of such a Confederation.

On 12 November 1953, however, in Paris, the General, after lamenting the failure of his original scheme for containing, by means of a Confederation, a divided Germany now, unhappily, established as an entity without any suitable "guarantees," and again denouncing the European Defence Community as a "trick" to get round the inevitable rearmament of "the Reich," says definitely that the latter should still "find her place" in a Confederation and that the UK should be in it too. However, the passage indicating this is followed by one which makes it clear that, in de Gaulle's view, the Atlantic Alliance should be revised so as to provide for the complete "independence" of its various members. One thing was certain: Britain would never have anything to do with the "European Army," which was true and had been demonstrated by the Tories when they returned to power at the end of 1951. Again, there is an expressed suspicion lest the arming of the Germans by the Americans should result eventually in some German hegemony over Europe.

In 1954 it is evident that the great decision on the EDC must shortly be taken. On 7 April, in Paris, de Gaulle therefore goes into battle, all guns firing, and it will be seen that the arguments employed in favour of his own counter-thesis are such as to appeal to most sections of French opinion—the extreme Right, the Federalists, the pro-British, even the Communists, could all derive some comfort. A great "plot," he said, was afoot to get France to agree to "total abdication." In Indo-China, in Germany, on the "European Army" she was being urged by sinister influences to compromise. But she should be strong enough by herself to influence both Super-Powers and thus prevent war. A "Europe" of "indestructible" nations, which can never be "merged," must now therefore be formed "from Gibraltar to the Urals and from Spitzbergen to Sicily." Charlemagne's Europe was no longer large enough.

Once again the notion of the "Confederation" —which should still include the UK—was outlined. Germany should of course be in it too with, however, special obligations and "*englobée*" by the other powers concerned. It was the thirtieth time since 1943, the General said, that he had put forward this particular conception. The speech ended with a final attack on the "monster" of the EDC and with a paean of praise for the French Empire. Some four months later the monster was dead, and in August a kind of war dance was executed by the General on its grave. He had of course been largely instrumental in the execution, and, indeed, looking back, it seems certain that, during the period 1950–54, most of his great energy was directed to this one end, or rather that all other foreign political conceptions on his part were subordinated to it. Anyhow, from August 1954 until he came into power in May 1958, the outpouring of ideas on Europe suddenly ceases. There is a growl about Germany in June 1955.[5] There is a reference, in

[5] "A re-armed Germany will always seek reunification and she may drag the West along with her in an attempt to force the Soviets to grant it, or she may turn to the East in order to buy it."

August 1956, to the danger of France's being drawn into "what are known as 'Communities'—either Atlantic or European—in which her independence, her personality and her soul might well disappear": a clear reference, no doubt, to the activities of Jean Monnet and the impending Treaties of Rome. But that is all. When I myself saw him during this period on 24 January 1957 and 20 March 1958, he was rather gloomy and quite accurately predicted that the long-term trend in Europe was towards the disruption of the two *blocs* and increasing independence on the part of the smaller allies. He also firmly maintained that Europe, or Western Europe, could not be formed as "a simple political entity." Monnet's views on all this were entirely unrealistic. Anyhow, there would be no World War, in all probability. The Russians were rapidly becoming quite "*embourgeoisés.*"

What conclusions can we, having heard the evidence, now draw as regards de Gaulle's known ideas about "Europe" when he was unexpectedly swept into power by the Algerian revolt? I think that they may be fairly summarized as follows:

(a) Until some time in 1949 the General genuinely believed that the main objective should be to form a "grouping" in Western Europe of which Britain and the Low Countries should be essential members and with which various autonomous German states might be associated in a rather subordinate capacity. The "grouping" might take the form of a "Federation," but this phrase was probably only adopted during this phase to please the resistants and the professional federalists. There was little doubt about where the General would wish the centre of this body to be or which country should take the initiative in its establishment.

(b) From late 1949 onwards de Gaulle, under the stress of the reconstitution of "the Reich" and its possible rearmament, recommended a very different policy, namely the construction of a "Federation" —later referred to as a "Confederation," but there is no apparent difference—which would be based on a Franco-German agreement. Britain might, in spite of grave doubts about whether she would, join such a Confederation—in fact up to 1954 at any rate the General seemed to think she could—but she would have to accept the fact that it would be entirely autonomous and that there would be no question of accepting any "Atlantic" or indeed "European" integration. Not to put too fine a point on it, there should be no longer any question of accepting an American Commander-in-Chief: SACEUR ought to be replaced by a French General, who would head the "Confederate" Army. No question, too, but that the centre of the proposed Confederation should be Paris, and that France should be the recognized leader of the whole outfit, Britain, after all, having the duty of organizing her Empire and Commonwealth, and more especially perhaps, pursuing her historic role in "l'Orient" (the Middle East).

(c) The intense hostility which the General manifested towards the EDC and, to a slightly lesser extent, towards the ECSC, was not so much directed against the EEC, which came into force, though not into full operation, some six months before he assumed power for the second time. Yet it was already clear from his attitude towards the ECSC that he was violently opposed to "integration" in any field, even more so to the principle of supra-nationality. Apart from the use of the terms "Federation" or "Confederation" (which in themselves could be twisted to mean almost anything) he had never departed from the essential principle, save only when, on one occasion, he referred to a possible partial delegation of sovereignty on the part of countries participating in his projected "grouping." But it was already obvious, from all his other published statements, that if anybody was going to renounce any portion of sovereignty that mattered it certainly would not be France.

Put in a more general way, de Gaulle's known European policy in 1958 may be said to have embodied three "constants." The essential, and indeed overriding one, was insistence on the absolute independence of France, whose "standing" or "status" (le rang) in the world was his main, some might even say it was his sole, political objective. Associated with this principle was the rejection of the slightest element of supra-nationality or "integration," by even small doses of which the French nation would inevitably be poisoned. And, lastly, there was the unshakable conviction that nothing which had been accomplished since the outbreak of the War without his personal participation was either useful or even valid, for France could, as he believed, only express herself through his person.

It follows that there was absolutely no excuse for anybody acquainted with the General's many utterances believing that his policy was not clear. It was all too clear. The only doubt might be on how, if at all, he would attempt to put his European principles into practice when he took over from the Fourth Republic. Many held that they were simply unrealizable dreams. What he did then we shall now examine.

3

Preparing the Way (1958-1963)

THE NEW Ruler did not, of course, seek immediately to apply a European policy different from that of his predecessors, and in any case he was probably quite happy with the way things were shaping. Though strongly opposed, as we have seen, to the supra-national element in the EEC, he had carefully refrained from attacking the latter directly. He had also, no doubt, already arrived at the conclusion that, since the Treaties of Rome had already been ratified by France, and had, indeed, actually come into force, and above all since the whole conception embodied his own basic idea of an ever-closer relationship between a re-vitalized France and a divided Germany, it would be best to let the Communities find their feet, trusting in his own ability eventually to shape them in accordance with his own nationalist convictions.

But this was for the future. When France agreed, some eight months after his assumption of power, to allow the EEC to come into force without applying the various "safeguards" for France negotiated by the Fourth Republic, the General instructed his Prime Minister, Michel Debré, to announce (on 15 January 1959) that "the Government will support the High Authority in its efforts to enforce respect for the letter and the spirit of the Treaty and, if necessary, will remind it of this obligation."[1] Besides, as a realist, and as a master of political tactics, de Gaulle knew that he must proceed slowly towards his objective. The Algerian war must evidently be ended before he

[1] Cf. the rather similar declaration of M. Couve de Murville on 13 October 1960: "There can be no question of France's creating an element of division within the Atlantic Alliance."

could take any new line, and it was to this end
that the greater part of his energies were from the
start directed. Four tedious years were to elapse
before the settlement came, and "Time's wingèd
chariot" became increasingly audible. How he eventually achieved that settlement is not part of this
story. As everybody knows, it was his greatest
claim to fame and something for which not only
France, but the whole of Europe, will be eternally
grateful to him. First, therefore, he had to establish
his own position, and as it were, clear the decks for
action. Nevertheless he could at least take certain preliminary steps to further his own European conceptions.

The first thing, evidently, was to establish a firm
working partnership with the "good German," recognized as such in March 1950, Konrad Adenauer. This
was not too easy. The "good German" was an anti-
militarist who had no liking for Generals. However,
at his first meeting with the Chancellor on 19 September 1958, at Colombey-les-deux-Eglises, de Gaulle
turned on his irresistible charm and an entente was
established which was never really broken, even when
Adenauer understood (as he did in September 1960)
that what he was being asked to accept was not
"Europe" after all, but a scheme for what might be
called a "Greater France." After all, Rhinelanders had
for many centuries looked to Paris as their cultural
centre; and to find a French General who was not only,
in principle, a Catholic but also an intellectual and,
over and above that, a man who understood Germany
and an undoubted leader of men, well, that was a
combination which few Rhinelanders could have re-

sisted. The provincial fell increasingly under the great man's spell, and one of the chief obstacles in the way of the realization of the "*vaste dessein*" was in this way largely avoided.

The next "interim" measure was to kill (unilaterally) the British plan to achieve a "European Industrial Free Trade Area." For there can be no doubt that, had that plan succeeded, the newly formed EEC would have been "merged in a greater whole" which, as de Gaulle saw it, could only lead to a Western "grouping" inevitably dominated by America. On 14 November, therefore, the French Minister of Information, Jacques Soustelle, was told to announce that France was no longer interested in the idea of a Free Trade Area; and it is worth while noting that this execution was approved not only by the German Chancellor at his second meeting with the General at Bad Kreutznach on 26 November, but by the German Finance Minister, Dr Erhard, who, up to that time, had been one of the Free Trade Area's foremost champions.

This was a shock for the British Government, though at this distance of time it is hard to understand how they could possibly have thought that their plan would succeed. It is probable that their negotiator, Reginald Maudling, able though he was, did not entirely grasp the political significance of the EEC. In any case his efforts to play off the Germans against the French were clearly doomed to failure. Moreover they aroused great, and it is to be feared, enduring suspicion of British motives among the members of the newly-formed European Commission in Brussels. Anyway, the die was now cast and British indignation at losing the role of economic leader of Western

Europe which had been theirs for ten years, found a
very natural expression in the formation, among the
"peripherals," of the European Free Trade Association.

There was another important initiative taken in
1958, and some hold—wrongly—that its failure resulted in both the moves so far noted. Wrongly,
because the first meeting with Adenauer had already
taken place and because there is no reason to suppose that the General, who had already decided to
accept the disciplines of the EEC (anyhow, for the
time being), could possibly have agreed to let France
enter into a Free Trade Area also. This was the
famous "Memorandum" communicated to the US and
British Governments on 16 September 1958. The full
text of this document has never been published officially, but no one doubts that it was on the lines of the
scheme outlined in August 1950 to which we have
already referred on page 34. In other words, the suggestion was that the USA, Britain and France should
agree to form what was virtually a "World Director-
ate" in which all major decisions affecting world
policy, including nuclear decisions, should be taken
only by common consent and that adequate machinery should be established for this purpose.

If carried to its logical conclusion, this would have
meant that France could exercise a veto on any major
move suggested by the United States. Even if it were
not to be taken literally, it meant that France would
be put in a much more favoured position as regards
consultations than, for example, Germany and Italy,
which was something that the US, as leaders of
the Atlantic Alliance, could not possibly accept. For

if they had accepted it, it would have meant that, in their view, France was able to speak for the entire Common Market—in other words, that the Market would be established on the basis of an acknowledged French leadership. This may well have been de Gaulle's intention, but he could hardly have seriously thought that the proposal could be accepted by America or even by Britain. As a matter of fact there is some reason to suppose that he did *not* mean it altogether seriously and merely put it forward for tactical purposes in order to make use of an expected rebuff to justify his later withdrawal from NATO.[2]

In any case the General's attitude towards military co-operation with the allies soon became abundantly clear and it would certainly have been made clear whether or not he had received any satisfaction as regards the "Memorandum." Speaking on 2 November 1959, at the Ecole Militaire in Paris (the scene of his dramatic triumph over his military contemporaries in 1927, when Pétain overruled the authorities and caused them to listen to a brilliant lecture by their unpopular subordinate), de Gaulle rejected any form of "integration" and insisted that "France would defend herself by herself, and in her own way." Her strategy could, of course, be co-ordinated with that of her allies at whose side, in case of real trouble, it was "infinitely probable" that France would be. But "integration" was inconceivable for her. In other words, if she could not be "integrated" in the Atlan-

[2] This, at any rate, is what Tournoux records the General as saying on p. 300 of *La Tragédie du Général*, and there is no doubt that in most of these recorded indiscretions Tournoux is by no means wide of the mark.

tic world, France was evidently not going to be "integrated" in Europe either.

The year 1959 was, however, not only clouded by the continuing war in Algeria, it also witnessed the Berlin crisis in East-West relations. Nikita Khrushchev's constant and expressed threat was that unless the Western Powers agreed to some new regime for Berlin the Russians would sign a Treaty handing over control of access to Berlin to the East Germans. An indecisive Foreign Ministers' meeting in 1959 and the abortive Summit meeting of May 1960 failed to break the common front of the Allies, and Khrushchev responded with the construction of the Berlin Wall on 13 August 1961. It was another year before he finally threw in the sponge over Cuba and the way was open for a real detente. These dates are important because they demonstrate that it was not before the end of 1962 (by which date the Algerian problem had also been solved) that de Gaulle was free to pursue an independent policy as regards both the Atlantic Alliance and Europe. It must also be recognized that throughout this crisis—as indeed over Cuba, too—de Gaulle's handling of Khrushchev was masterly. He was convinced that Stalin's successor would never press his demands to the point of actually risking war with America, and events proved him right. But it must now be seen that one of his main objects in pursuing this tough line was to retain the confidence of the Germans and, notably, of Chancellor Adenauer.

One obvious result of the torpedoing of the general European Free Trade Area idea, however, was to cause Britain to reflect very seriously on her whole future position. Her previous constant hostility to the whole idea of a Customs Union made it difficult for her to switch over abruptly and apply for membership of the EEC. Yet there was a risk that the obvious success of the EEC, combined with the "Summit" fiasco of 1960 might induce America no longer to consider Britain as a "special partner," but rather the Community, which could even one day become one of the Great Powers of the world. Hence it became clear to a highly intelligent British Prime Minister that Britain had no choice. It would have been better if he and his party had reached this conclusion rather earlier; but even in July 1961, when the British asked for negotiations for entry, the General was, for him, in a rather weak position.

In the first place, the Algerian war, disastrous for France, showed no signs of ending. In the second place he had by no means succeeded in converting even his own adherents to his (as yet undeclared) new policy, namely, to form a Western European "Confederation" led by France, without Britain, and then to work for the dissolution of NATO, though not necessarily the Western Alliance, in order to negotiate a German, and indeed a general European settlement direct with the Soviet Union. Indeed, if he had at this stage declared that this really was his idea he might have encountered insuperable resistance. At that stage, for instance, it was essential for him to keep certain "Europeans" in his Cabinet. Nor was it possible to go beyond a certain point in conversations with Adenauer. France had not built up sufficient financial reserves to maintain any genuinely independent policy. She had not, for that matter, any nuclear force —of strictly limited use for defence of course, but of considerable importance for prestige and propaganda. In any case, as we have just seen, there was, as yet, no detente which could facilitate an independent policy. Lastly, it was still rather an early stage in the wooing of Germany. Moreover, to admit "*L'Angleterre*" into the Common Market, before France had established a clear ascendancy, would obviously frustrate his entire policy. For either in that event the leadership of the new "Confederation" would have to be collective—an intolerable thought, and one contrary to all his principles—or Britain would, as he saw it, be the "Trojan Horse" which would transform the Common Market into an "Atlantic Community." It was necessary to go slow, to disguise his thought, as he very skilfully did during his extremely successful visit to London in April 1960; to escape slowly from the Atlantic "integration" which, as he believed, was restricting the freedom of action of France; to make renewed efforts to get together with the Germans; and above all, to end the Algerian war. It was necessary, too, to liquidate the old French Empire, which he did with consummate skill, retaining much more influence for France in Africa than Britain did in her corresponding exercise in disengagement.

It was also necessary to rally the Six so far as possible to his general conception of Europe and thus prepare the way for his "Confederation." Meanwhile, how should political co-operation best be organized? Everyone agreed that, now that the Community was working, the first steps should be taken. The evident opinion of the "Five" was that this should, as it were, grow out of the EEC and that the same sort of techniques as were being elaborated in the Community should be gradually adopted in the political sphere as well; in other words that, so proceeding, they would eventually arrive at a Federation, or its equivalent, and hence at the creation of one European entity and not at a collection of sovereign European States.

This was the reverse of the conception of the General. We have already seen how (except on one occasion which was obviously a mistake or an effort to get over an immediate hurdle) he had never deviated from the following sequence of thought. Nations, and more particularly the French nation, are the product of centuries, sometimes millennia, of growth and cannot therefore be abolished, "merged" or even restricted in the full exercise of their complete independence, except by an act of force. Even if they are physically suppressed for a time they tend to recover their "individuality." Nevertheless "Europe," in the sense of the various European nations of East and West, has a vital role to play in the world and must come together and speak with one voice if domination by one Super-Power or the other is to be avoided. Therefore, there is only one solution: they must all come together under the aegis of France, the most ancient, the most central and, it must be recognized, the most civilized of all the European countries. There is no other solution, and time presses. In shorthand, the expression commonly used to denote this conception is a "*Europe des Patries,*" or, as the General himself insists, a "Europe of States."

In the summer of 1960—one year before Britain's application—Alain Peyrefitte, then a Gaullist deputy, circulated a confidential memorandum on the tactics that the French Government might be well advised to follow. The contents were indeed enlightening. "The importance of the psychological difficulties which the European Plan of General de Gaulle presents for our neighbours should not put us off: but it does necessitate a tactical manoeuvre." The French should consequently at all costs avoid being thought "negative." They should show without ambiguity (a) that their attitude towards European institutions was constructive and that they had no desire to dismantle the Communities, but rather to perfect them: (b) that they were not opposed *a priori* to the prolongation of the Treaties of Rome and Paris: (c) that the French position as regards the British problem was "conciliatory and pragmatic": and (d) that France was ready to go very far, when circumstances so permitted, in the Confederal direction already indicated.

Presented with "all the seduction inherent in the possibility of their renewal," such French initiatives should make it clear that of all the Europeans the French were those most anxious to proceed towards the union of Europe. ". . . Let us even let our partners believe, or pretend to believe, that the President of the Republic and the French Government have been converted to their theses." In this way boring and profitless debates would be avoided. This would also be the way "to wrap up the Communities in a political system which, by gradually defining their competence, will protect them from their own political initiatives." All this would be the easier because, in practice, supranationality was "already dead," and its advocates, whether national or individual, only pretended to believe in it in order to paddle their own canoes. The

Commission might become rather obstreperous, but its members could always in the last resort be kept in order by a frank private talk between a French Minister and the erring Member or Members. Besides, all the Members of the EEC were only "Community-minded" when it suited them. Many quite disputable instances were given.

The paper continued at length in this vein. The whole question was how best to give some lip service to the idea of a "European Community" while actually developing the system of a "Europe of States." Much play was made with "the importance of not being shown to wish to exclude the British while at the same time adopting the British formula," i.e. a non-supra-national Community. It was true that "no solid European construction can at present be undertaken together with Great Britain." But it was also true that "the Europe that we [the French] wish to construct is identical with what the United Kingdom has been advocating ever since 1948." It was evident, on the one hand, that Britain must not be allowed in "in the first stage" (presumably, that is, before a political Europe had been established) but to reject her out of hand might have very unfortunate results on the Partners. France should therefore appear to be the great champion of the Community and the Five should be brought to believe that only by excluding Britain could the latter be gradually forced to accept Community conditions. After all, it was only the formation of the EEC which had resulted so far in a seeming change of attitude on her part. If France indeed was sufficiently "audacious" it might well be that Britain would be forced. as it were, to exclude herself. That would be perfect. The paper ended by suggesting, prophetically enough, that the best way to put French political ideas across would be to organize a triumphal tour of Germany by the General. This was the background against which the latter proceeded to take the next steps towards the creation of his "Confederation."[3]

The first was, not unnaturally, to sell his conception finally to Chancellor Adenauer, whom he had been seeing regularly since the dramatic first meeting in September 1958. But at the meeting at Rambouillet on 29 July 1960 things appear to have gone slightly wrong. When the aged Chancellor got home, indeed, his officials pointed out to him what the effect on the whole Brussels organization would be if the General's political proposals—aimed precisely at dominating this machine and rendering it powerless by subjecting it to a non-supra-national political body—were accepted. For the first time, according to Roger Massip[4]—to whose excellent analysis I am much indebted in the ensuing passage—the personal relationship between the two great men underwent what might indeed be called a crisis. Undaunted, the General pursued his well-known line.

On 5 September 1960, at one of the Press Conferences which were now becoming one of his favourite

[3] It was true that the idea of periodic meetings of Foreign Ministers had been mooted at his meeting with the Italian President in August 1959 and had actually been agreed to at Strasbourg in November of that year. But these were simple exchanges of view. Now it was a question of finding out how political decisions might be taken, which was something very different.

[4] *De Gaulle et l'Europe*, Flammarion, 1963.

political weapons, he spoke his mind quite clearly. The only "reality" in Europe, he predictably declared, was the State. To think you could build on anything else was a "chimaera." It was true that certain "extra-national" organizations had been created which had a certain technical value but could never possess any authority. Only States could take decisions, however, and the only way by which they could arrive at such decisions was by *co-operation*, to be achieved by "a regular and organized concert of the responsible governments" assisted by "specialized organisms" and by a Parliament not elected but nominated from among members of national Parliaments. The whole scheme would be set on foot as the result of a referendum. This was what France proposed and (rather forgetting Peyrefitte's cunning advice) de Gaulle let it be understood that there was no other way and that his hearers could take it or leave it.

This pronouncement had a fairly hostile reception, but in order to make at least some progress the Five agreed with the General's proposal to hold a Summit Conference, and two such Conferences were, in fact, held during 1961, on 10 February in Paris and on 19 July in Bonn. The first did not get very far, but it was agreed that the French might put up a definite draft agreement. The Five were concerned at this point to make it clear that no new political institutions should be allowed to weaken the supra-national character of the existing institutions and this was agreed. At the second Summit the French dropped the idea of a referendum and no longer insisted on periodic meetings of Defence Ministers which, so the Five believed, might cut across NATO obligations. Indeed an allusion to the reinforcement of the Atlantic Alliance was actually inserted in the draft. On the other hand a Commission of Experts was set up in Paris to prepare and submit a final draft. This became known as the "Fouchet Commission" and it duly produced the famous "Fouchet Plan."

The main features of the original Fouchet Plan were as follows. The new institution would cover foreign policy, defence and cultural matters. A Council would meet no fewer than six times a year either at Head of Government or at Foreign-Minister level. For at least three years it would take decisions by unanimous vote (abstentions discounted). It would be assisted by a "Political Commission" consisting of high officials. A common Assembly with that of the existing organizations would only have limited powers. The draft was at once criticized by the Parliament of Europe on the grounds that it embodied the principle of the veto; that the powers of the projected Assembly were much too limited (it could not even pass a vote of censure on the Council); that the Political Commission would simply take its orders from the respective governments and thus in no way be comparable to the Brussels Commission; and that there was no guarantee in the "revision clause" that this nationalist set-up would not last for as long as the Treaty.

Still, it looked as if the French proposal would have gone through had it not been for a last-minute intervention, early in January 1962, by the General, the substance of whose proposed amendments was to the effect that the existing (Brussels) Commissions should "lose their autonomy"; that the organs of the Common Market should be "rationalized" after a certain period; that the new Council should, after all, deal with economic matters; that no reference be made to the Atlantic Alliance in connection with defence; that the role of the Assembly should be yet further reduced, and that there should be no provision in the "revision clause" that existing institutions would be respected. The intention was absolutely clear. It was to subject to the will of France, and hence to emasculate, the communal institutions of the Common Market. All this was reinforced by a "Press Conference" on 5 February in which de Gaulle justified the scrapping of integration by the necessity of "bringing Europe out of the realm of ideology and technology and into that of reality, that is to say of politics." Perhaps. But it was a question also of bringing France back into the system of simple "co-operation" between sovereign nations which had involved her three times in 150 years in total defeat and had plunged the whole Continent into calamity after calamity.

Astonishingly enough, when a few days later de Gaulle again met the Chancellor he was as well received as ever. Clearly touched, he even agreed to two modifications, namely a reference, after all, to the Atlantic Alliance and an admission that the new Council could not decide on economic matters though it might, periodically, discuss them—a rather dangerous distinction without much difference, one would have thought. He also flew to Turin in a snowstorm in order to try to bring Fanfani into line. Such was the desire of the Five to achieve some rudimentary political organization that they would probably have agreed in April 1962 even to the revised French text —the only outstanding issue then being French insistence on retaining a revision clause which contained no allusion to a possible advance towards a real political union—but for a new element in the situation.

Speaking officially on behalf of Her Majesty's Government, Edward Heath declared on 9 April that Britain, who had applied to join the EEC seven months previously, was prepared, for her part, to assume all the political obligations of the Treaty of Rome. Her Majesty's Government also suggested that they might profitably be associated with the consultations on political union. The Dutch and the Belgians promptly maintained that if they were to accept the French draft it could only be when Britain became a member of the Community. A "Europe of States" would be a poor thing and quite intolerable on Gaullist terms since it would imply the end of the Brussels machine and the institution of a French hegemony. But with Britain one thing at least would be certain: hegemony could not be exercised by any one power and moreover Britain had said that she, for her part, accepted the Community system. On 17 April, therefore, the "Fouchet Plan" collapsed, very probably because de Gaulle, alarmed at the prospect of British participation in the talks, no longer desired further progress. It was on 18 April, in any case, that feelers were put out for an exchange of visits with the Germans at the highest level.

On 15 May, de Gaulle pronounced a sort of funeral oration. The EEC, he rightly remarked, could not for long continue without some political organization. But the United Kingdom would never agree to "dissolve itself in some Utopian construction." The national feeling which had given birth to Dante, Goethe and Chateaubriand, but not, it would appear, to Shakespeare, must continue. The only way in which a Federation could be achieved would be by a "Federator"—an outside one presumably—and no Federator was present. As for the Council of Europe, it was destined, to quote Racine, to "die on the shores where it had been abandoned." The MRP members of the Government, who had only joined it ten days previously, promptly resigned; but attention was now focused on the great struggle attendant on the first effort of the United Kingdom to join the Common Market. And it was about then too, that some "Elysée-ölogists" became convinced that the General was resolved to exclude Britain if humanly possible.

The history of these negotiations cannot concern us here except insofar as they make clear the "European" intentions of General de Gaulle. It is true that this astute man had not actually declared his fundamental hostility to British entry as soon as the decision to apply for membership had been made. On the contrary he stated on 6 September 1961 that he had no objection to this as such, provided only that Britain was able to accept all the provisions of the Treaty of Rome. But nobody who knew him at all well, or had followed his pronouncements, could possibly have imagined that he would in any circumstances actually welcome British entry. Indeed, on the last time on which I saw him officially before my retirement from the Foreign Service in September 1960, he had made it clear, in answer to a direct question, that he did not think, in view of our Commonwealth commitments, that we could possibly join the EEC, anyhow for a considerable time. In late 1962, however, he was, frankly, not strong enough, either internally or externally, to go so far as to veto negotiations as he found it possible to do just over six years later.

In the light of all this, even if we ignore subsequent developments, there can surely now be no doubt that the General was determined from the beginning to do his best to block the entry of the United Kingdom into the EEC. It is true that in March 1961, Couve de Murville had been allowed to make certain agreeable, even if non-committal, noises regarding a possible British entry; but that was at a moment when it was important from the French point of view that too much progress should not be made with EFTA and in the prospective negotiations for general tariff reduction. It was important that the Six should make progress on agricultural policy first. Nor was there, as is sometimes suggested, any "green light" when de Gaulle met Macmillan in November 1961 at the latter's country house in Sussex. Most of the discussions were on Berlin and on his return to Paris the General is said to have reported to the Germans with considerable effect on what he held to be the weak-kneed attitude of the British Government. It is arguable that had the British Government accepted by the end of the summer of 1962 the sort of economic conditions that they seemed willing to accept five years later; had they, in addition, been prepared to agree that the Community should, in principle, be entirely independent of America and eventually dependent only on its own arms for its own defence; had they, more especially, agreed to help the General in his nuclear projects, it would have been difficult for him to have put a sudden end to the negotiations. Perhaps he might even have been forced to accept some kind of "delayed entry" for Britain into the Common Market.

What exactly happened at the Conference of the Château de Champs, in June 1962, between Macmillan and the President may never be revealed; but the French have continued ever since to drop hints that there was then some hope of an agreement. It is possible that Georges Pompidou, who had newly arrived on the scene, was anxious that the General should not give the impression that he was unalterably opposed to British entry in any circumstances and that the "atmosphere" was thus allowed to be "cordial." But that was probably all. In the light of what happened subsequently any other hypothesis seems entirely improbable.

The fact was that towards the end of 1962, the President, in his own belief at any rate, had at last "freed his hands." The revolt of the French Generals in Algiers had been smashed in April 1961. The final agreement with the Algerians themselves had been concluded at Evian in March 1962. De Gaulle, by an absolute miracle, which must have proved to him that he was the Man of Destiny, had escaped assassination at Petit-Clamart in August. Cuba was presaging a detente. In July there had been the great State Visit of Adenauer to France. Together the two leaders had reviewed troops on the historic fields of Champagne; together they had knelt before the High Altar of Reims Cathedral. In September there had been the triumphal return tour of the French President in Germany. The twelve-year-long courtship of the Fatherland was nearing its end. "*Sie sind ein grosses Volk,*" the General told the enraptured multitude. Both the French and the German nations, he informed the Hamburg Military Academy, had owed much to their respective armies. Sowing the wind? Perhaps, but the great thing was the immediate goal. If he could bring off some special arrangement with the Germans of a political nature based on the principle of the independent Nation State, that would be the basis for his own kind of Europe and the other grumbling partners would just have to come along and accept it.

In a sense, therefore, the Franco-German Treaty of the following January would be, so to speak, an *Ersatz*-Fouchet. It is true that even on his return from his visit he had considerable qualms. His proposal for a Franco-German plebiscite had been turned down by Adenauer who had also made it clear that he could not be expected to break completely with America. It was about now, therefore, always according to Tournoux, that he said in private conversation that it was just not true that the Germans were "a great people." If they had been, they would never have received him as they did! No matter: he had above all to try to accomplish the *"vaste dessein"* to which he had been called by Providence. As an enthusiastic German newspaper remarked, de Gaulle had come to Germany as the King of France and had returned to Paris as the Emperor of Europe. That at least this apotheosis was unlikely was no doubt the canker in the rose.

Two matters remained, however, to be settled before he could indeed have a free hand to pursue his objective. After Petit-Clamart he had decided, illegally, as most lawyers would argue, to revise the Constitution by referendum so as to provide for the election of the President of France by direct rather than by indirect suffrage. The implications of this Bonapartist man-oeuvre were obvious enough, but it had to be accepted by the country. It was, by a large majority, at the end of October. The only remaining hurdle was that of the Parliamentary elections in November. Many Frenchmen had predicted that the General, summoned to power to solve an almost insoluble problem, would somehow be put back to grass when it was out of the way. Not so. The elections, to the surprise of many Gaullists, resulted in a clear majority for the General. There was now no possibility, for some five years, of any vote of censure on the President's Government and he had the power to nominate as Prime Minister anybody of his choosing. He was in complete control of the country, and it only remained to pass from words to deeds.

The way was thus clear for Rambouillet. Here General de Gaulle, for the first time, came out clearly, even if not absolutely, against British entry and maintained that the negotiations had proved that Britain could not, for the time being at any rate, fulfil the necessary economic conditions of entry, notably as regards agriculture. Yet the report of the Brussels Commission showed that the admittedly major difficulties could have been solved in continuing negotiations. If he meant that Britain, once in the EEC, would not agree that it should sever all links with America, this was true; but neither could the other EEC partners and a substantial section of French public opinion. If Macmillan hinted at the possibility of a joint Anglo-French nuclear programme within a Union of Western Europe—as he may have done at Champs—he must have linked it with a scheme which made it compatible with the North Atlantic Alliance, something which the General could never accept. But when subsequently Macmillan agreed at Nassau that British nuclear submarines should be provided with Polaris missiles, subject to their forming part of an Atlantic force, de Gaulle, even though he was offered the same facilities, was provided with a heaven-sent opportunity to break. For President Kennedy's extended offer to France was irrelevant in the context of de Gaulle's principle of total national independence, notwithstanding the fact that France had not as yet any nuclear submarines in which to house the Polaris weapons. And the General was in any case now powerful enough to torpedo Kennedy's "Grand Design."

So the first two "deeds" of the new policy were soon apparent. They consisted, in January 1963, in throwing Britain out of "Europe" and in signing the Franco-German Treaty. It is true that, in the interval, there was the curious incident connected with the Russian Ambassador in Paris who was summoned to the Elysée and given to understand that the General would still prefer to do a separate deal with the USSR—an idea which the Soviet Government promptly rejected. But the important point was that by mid-December the General had finally "freed his hands." In other words, the fate of the long-drawn-out negotiations in Brussels had already by then been determined. "Mon ami, M. Macmillan" ("un Anglais de grande distinction" in the Gaullist hierarchy) never really had a chance.

4

First Efforts to Apply the Plan (1963-1966)

THUS, AT the end of January 1963, the ball, in theory, was at the General's feet. The Algerian war was over: the French economy was forging ahead: the English rival had been kept out of "Europe": the "special relationship" with Germany had, at any rate on paper, been achieved. Now presumably was the moment to press ahead with the "vast plan," with the long-term objective, that is, of rallying "the Gauls, the Latins, the Teutons and the Slavs," the "Anglo-Saxon" provincials being duly relegated, for a long time at any rate, to the world periphery. The concept of the "Nation-State" must also be vaunted as the basis of all international dealings and thus France would always, and in any circumstances, preserve her freedom of action.

Once progress had been made towards a European "Confederation" centred on Paris there would be no further need for an American military presence in Europe. It would still be useful, no doubt, to maintain the Atlantic Alliance. In a general way it might be desirable to be able to invoke the threat of American nuclear power for the defence of Europe if the Soviet Union should show signs of resuming an aggressive policy. But NATO, i.e. the "integrated" arm of the Alliance, should be dismantled. For it could, by the force of things, only be based on an American hegemony which it was de Gaulle's declared object to eliminate. Besides, he was right in thinking that, in spite of the warnings which he had received, the EEC would survive the crisis which followed his first veto. There was, indeed, a crisis of confidence; but the interest of the Five in maintaining the Brussels machinery was predictably greater than their will to bring any serious pressure to bear on the General to reverse his policy. To that extent the ground in Germany had been well prepared. Nor was the British reaction anything save completely passive.

Things hardly worked out this way. We have noted that even at the moment of his triumph, on returning from his tour of Germany in September, the President may well have felt that he was unlikely to carry that country with him in his "vast plan." It was pretty clear that if they were absolutely forced to choose between France and the United States the Germans would opt for America. After all, only a few days after the signature of the Treaty on 22 January 1963, the German Government expressed, in Brussels, their opposition to the rupture with the United Kingdom and their continued desire for British entry. The gesture did not amount to much in practice, but in May the Bundestag added a Preamble to the Franco-German Treaty which, from the General's point of view, nullified its whole intention—that the Bundesrepublik should break with America and choose France as her principal partner and protector. From then on, until the departure from power of Erhard in October 1966, de Gaulle became increasingly anti-German, or at least anti-Bonn, the signing of the Test Ban Treaty by the West German Government being the final straw. The German leaders, he said, were "poor types," the Federal Republic "a broken-backed State,"[1] which was quite unable to resist American hegemony.

Besides, after the end of 1962, the idea of a "Multi-

[1] Tournoux, op. cit., p. 463.

lateral Nuclear Force" (mentioned in the Nassau agreement) began to be put about by the Americans after a preliminary tour of Europe by its originator, Livingston Merchant. This project for a fleet of nuclear submarines assigned to NATO which would be jointly financed, manned and commanded was evidently intended to square the circle as regards the presumed desire of the Germans to take a more active part in policy, and notably in atomic policy, while maintaining the treaty obligation on the Federal Republic not to manufacture or possess atomic weapons of any sort. It was a policy only with difficulty reconcilable with the East/West detente; but the Americans were keener at that moment on conciliating the Germans than on pleasing the Russians. As for the General, he is believed to have told the Germans that he would break with them altogether if they joined. Weakened by British proposals for an "Atlantic Nuclear Force" the project nevertheless dragged on, and was finally killed by President Johnson himself in December 1964. The act of the President did more, perhaps, to draw the Germans over to the French side than anything else.

The other, and even more absorbing question to occupy the attention of the General during this phase was agriculture, that is to say, French agriculture, and here he made use of his excellent civil servants to get the best possible terms for France. Since it had been part of the original bargain which produced the EEC that France should be expected to open up her internal market for industrial goods to European competition in return for special arrangements for the disposal within the Common Market of her large agricultural surpluses, he also had, broadly speaking, the Brussels Commission on his side. In battle after battle—for, after all, the French price was a high one for their partners to pay, and alienating the affections of farmers, however inefficient, is a pretty risky political operation—the French, in general, prevailed, and at the end of 1964, at a "marathon" session in Brussels of the Council of Ministers, the great decision was taken on the Common Market price for grain. Given German opposition, the price, however, was far higher than it should have been, and calculated to maintain the inefficient farmer to the general detriment of the Community, thus producing unmanageable surpluses. But it did clear the way for an agreement on the financing of the entire policy and this therefore was what the Commission began to prepare at the beginning of 1965.

The crisis following the Commission's proposals in March of that year is very relevant to our story. The Commission's plan was one which, in the last resort, and as the result of a complicated procedure, would have allowed the decision on the disposal of the enormous proceeds of the "levies" on imported foodstuffs to be taken by a "qualified" (or weighted) majority vote in the Council of Ministers and by a special vote in the so-called Parliament of Europe. This plan, it should be emphasized, was only put forward as a basis for discussion and was in entire accordance with the principles embodied in the Treaty of Rome and notably the rule whereby weighted majority voting in the Council was to come into force legally at the end of the Third Phase of the application of the Treaty, namely on 1 January 1966. But, if adopted, it would have meant that the French Government would no longer have been able, in the last resort, to impose a veto on any proposal within the sphere of the Treaty to which it objected on purely national grounds.

The General decided to act. At the end of June he withdrew the French Delegation from Brussels and France, so to speak, went on strike. In January 1966 it was agreed, at Luxemburg, that France could return to the fold with the nominal powers of the Commission only slightly curbed but on the agreed assumption that, while the Five would respect their legal obligations regarding majority voting, France would not necessarily do so if she declared that her "vital interests" were at stake. In other words, France was successful in getting the Five to recognize, in practice, and for the time being, her right of veto. But the general principle of majority voting was preserved and is, in practice, often now applied. Small wonder, however, that, after this tearing up of the Treaty of Rome by one of the signatories much of the original impetus departed from the Community. The collective idea persisted but there was an increasing tendency to discuss major problems first of all among the national delegations. It represented, in fact, the first significant step away from an incipient organic union and towards the famous "Europe of States."

The tendency was probably strengthened by the French withdrawal from NATO (though not from the Alliance) which took place three months after the "compromise" of Luxemburg. Again, this decision rent the EEC. The Germans, in particular, were faced with the terrible dilemma of having to separate themselves either from the Americans or from the French. It would have been different, perhaps, if some years before, a European Political Union had been established which included the United Kingdom. But de Gaulle, by insisting on his "Fouchet" plan for a French hegemony and by excluding Britain had, as we have already seen, unfortunately made this impossible. With many groans, therefore, the Germans "chose America," while agreeing to the maintenance of French troops on their soil, and the General retaliated by seeming to choose the Soviet Union. We shall come to the Russian visit later. But it is against this background that we may now examine how de Gaulle developed his European theses during what I have called his first effort to apply "the Plan" insofar as there was now a consistent effort to do so.

Soon after the first veto, then, we learn that "in order to make Europe, Germany must be 'anchored.'" She is "the base of Europe." For her part Britain, "if she ever has to choose between Europe and the open sea she will choose the open sea." These words, spoken by the General in Paris on 24 January 1963, undoubtedly reveal his sincere belief. They were spoken, be it noted, two days after the signature of the Franco-German Treaty, and they came, as it were, from the depths. He really did, he really does, believe that Germany is the key to the solution of the European problem and that Britain is simply not in a position to turn the key. It is true that soon after the Veto—on 12 February—he said that "Britain could come into the Common Market one day if she wanted to," and, indeed, that he hoped that "one day she might enter the EEC—on conditions." But these were obviously attempts to appease those who had been outraged by his individual action and designed to tide him over a rather awkward period. The authentic note was struck again on 5 February, in Paris, when it was alleged that "America, making use of Britain, is trying to set up a huge contraption of Free Trade with the Irish, the Icelanders, etc.," and on 23 April, at Rethel, when we hear that "Europe must be formed and France must be at the head of it." This note was also struck all through an extensive tour of the Champagne country during that month, in the course of which de Gaulle referred to the necessity of constructing the Political Community of the future. Nations must, of course, remain nations but there was no reason why they could not have a "common world policy," "a common defence," and so on. In fact, the pure milk of the "Fouchet Plan."[2]

The point was made even more clearly on 19 April 1963, in Paris. "Any system which consisted of handing over our sovereignty to international '*aréopages*'[3] would be incompatible with the rights and duties of the French Republic." He wanted to see Europe formed "by those nations which had the genuine will and ability to belong to it," including, perhaps, one day, "the great English people," though meanwhile the latter would have to develop in "their own way." In this summer, in a tour of south-west France, a new note creeps in to his many speeches on European matters. One of the main reasons, it seems, for creating any European Union is to increase aid to underdeveloped countries, "the hungry milliards." During

[2] See page 69.
[3] Areopagus, the ancient Athenian Court of Justice.

this tour also we even hear references to the Atlantic Alliance, but only to justify the creation of Europe as "an equal ally" of the United States of America, the Franco-German Treaty being the foundation of "Europe." Europe itself "will be constructed like a State, like a nation," and not in accordance with "dreams that have no connection with reality."

Nothing could possibly have been clearer. Besides, he confidently asserted, "Europe" had now understood. First the EEC must develop and a Political Community must arise out of it. First Western Europe must be constructed on this basis and then there might be "a detente extending from the Atlantic to the Urals, perhaps even an entente, perhaps even, eventually, a co-operation," a conception of which we shall hear much more later.

The essential independence of France was the theme of a policy statement in July. The increasing difficulties of the Americans with their balance of payments made their desire that France should merge herself in a vague "Atlantic Community" comprehensible. But (Franco-German) Europe would not lend itself to any such thing, all the more so since it ought to be as nearly self-sufficient in foodstuffs as possible—autarkic it might almost be said. Independence was likewise the theme of the autumn tour of 1963. France was a member of NATO, of the United Nations, and of Europe. But in all these bodies she remained herself and her essential integrity was in no way affected by membership. It was evident that, as de Gaulle saw it, there was no essential difference between membership of the first two of these organizations and the last. That the European Economic Community had certain original features; that there were legal obligations on France to abide by its terms and notably to acknowledge the very real powers conferred on the Commission and the obligation to accept (in certain very rare cases) majority verdicts, was something which he just could not admit. He appears to have regarded them throughout as strange phantasies which were somehow accepted by the rulers of France at a moment when "France" was not fully awake and aware of what was being imposed on her by the foreigners.

This note was still dominant at the end of 1963 when France was already enjoying considerable success in the community's agricultural negotiations. "It is a fact," the General remarked "that in endeavouring to put our relations with Germany on a new footing, in seeing to it that the EEC is really a Community and really European including agriculture as well as industry, not dissolved by the admission of a new member who cannot accept the rules, nor annexed to the system prevailing on the other side of the Atlantic, we have been largely instrumental in forming the Common Market and thus in freeing the way that leads to a United Europe." So France was now working on "three great tasks": the Union of the Six in the sphere of politics, defence and culture; progress with the under-developed countries, "above all those in Africa"; and lastly, the maintenance of peace. On this last point it was essential that France should provide herself with a thermonuclear bomb, the only weapon which would give her real "independence." It was necessary too, to assist "our Western Europe, as soon as it is united," to establish "a political, economic and strategic entente" with America. Last, but not least, it was necessary "to contemplate an evolution of the totalitarian Communist regimes in Warsaw, Prague, Pankow, Budapest, Bucharest, Sofia, Belgrade, Tirana and Moscow in a way corresponding to our own transformation." (The key word here was "Pankow." Notice was given that if the Germans—still in disgrace—could not see the light, some suitable arrangement might nevertheless be arrived at with the unmentionable East Berlin authorities.) Only then, the General concluded, would there be "possibilities for the whole of Europe which would correspond to its resources and capacities."

On 31 January 1964 de Gaulle drew certain conclusions from the French agricultural victory of the previous month. The great thing about this event, he argued, was that it proved that what he called "Economic Europe" had the will to live. Of course much had been scribbled over the years in the capitals of the Six about the advantages of a European Economic Community, but in order to achieve this in practice it was necessary to leave the "fairy kingdom of speculation" and enter the world of "harsh reality." Naturally the details of the arrangements reached had been prepared by technicians, but actual decisions could only be taken by States. The Brussels Commission had done work of great value, but it was left to the governments to face their responsibilities. Thus, however excellent the labours of the Commission, it was quite wrong to label it an "Executive." It was nothing of the sort. It was simply a meeting of international experts.

De Gaulle also seized this occasion to elaborate his thought in general on how the Community should function correctly. So far as industry was concerned, he maintained, there was no essential difficulty; but if agriculture had not been taken into due account, France would have had to withdraw from the Common Market. But Germany had played the game, and de Gaulle paid tribute to Erhard's "fidelity." All the same, political co-operation was necessary to protect Europe from disruptive forces from within and without. Adenauer had shown the way by signing the Franco-German Treaty but this example had not been followed up.

There had been objections that any political union must be supra-national; that it must not be formed without Britain; that in any case it should form part of an "Atlantic Community." All these objections were contradictory and the first was impossible. Britain, which was a great nation, would accept such a solution least of all.

But it was now, under the influence of his German disappointment, that de Gaulle took up the Third World in a big way. We have already seen how it began to creep into his speeches during the spring of 1964. Now it became a theme. The chief point, almost, of "Europe" was to bring aid and comfort to "the starving milliards." Naturally it would be France who would take the lead in this direction, but aid would not now only be directed towards the ex-French Colonies. No, there were wider perspectives. The rulers of Cambodia and of Laos were mentioned in the 21 January Press Conference; but above all Latin America beckoned. France was calling in the New World to impose her balance on the old. In March the General left for Mexico: in the autumn he was to visit all the more important capitals of Latin America. André Fontaine says,[4] somewhat unkindly, that the main object was to give de Gaulle the opportunity to "revel in adulation" and to satisfy his almost physical need to "mingle" with as large a crowd as possible. There is no doubt something in this, but the main object of these journeys was undoubtedly political. It is true that when I saw him in September 1964, just before his departure for South America, he minimized the importance of this aspect to me; but on the whole I agree with Alfred Grosser that the main reason for his preoccupation with the sufferings of the "Third World" was to arrive by another way at the same goal: France, the leader of "Europe" would be able to speak as an equal in the councils of the Super-Powers.

Basic disappointment with Germany was the main characteristic of the General's attitude towards Europe in 1964. There was a strong grumble from him in Bonn itself on 4 July. The day must come, he asserted, when the two countries had a common foreign policy, but that day was evidently not yet. On 23 July, in a Press Conference in Paris, we had a really brilliant description of his general point of view. After the war America and Russia were, from the point of view of world power, alone: the conquered were wallowing in their total defeat; the "European conquerors," presumably France and Britain, were "profoundly undermined." It was thus inevitable that the New World, strong in the possession of the atom bomb, should protect the Old, distribute Marshall Aid, organize general security everywhere (NATO, CENTO, SEATO, OAS and—indirectly—the UN): insist on

[4] *Foreign Affairs*, October 1967.

the liquidation of the old European Empires, ending up with Suez; counter Soviet expansion in Korea and in the Congo and, generally, run the world. But now, nearly twenty years later, all had changed. The Western States of "our old Continent" had rebuilt their economies and their military forces. One of them, France, had become a nuclear power as well. They had, further, "become aware of their natural links." In short, "Western Europe" appeared capable of becoming a "first-class entity" [*entité capitale*], capable of living its own life, not, indeed, in opposition to the New World, but alongside it. On the other side the monolith of the totalitarian world was cracking up. A huge, uncertain China had appeared on the scene, while the Empire of the Soviet Union—the last of the great colonial powers—was being confronted not only by China but by the European satellites. Even in Russia itself, and in spite of the enormous effort put into certain large-scale constructions, the Communist regime had failed, in respect of the standard of living and the dignity of man, to equal the system applied in the West which was partly directed and partly free. The Third World, likewise, was being shaken by tremendous difficulties.

It was thus obvious that the "two camps" system had, in effect, disappeared and that Europe, if she so desired, had a great role to play—a Europe still allied to America but helping her, as an equal, to carry out her world responsibilities. That was why the Americans themselves wanted Europe to be formed and why "among the Gauls, the Latins, and the Germans" the cry went up, "Let us make Europe." But what Europe? The French wanted a European Europe, and one which, "in the middle of the world," was able to apply her own policy. But others did not really want this, and consciously or unconsciously, would prefer to be subject to American "leadership." That was why they proposed a "Federal" Europe, the well-known *"aréopage"* with its Executive and its Legislature. But the defect was that such a set-up could not possibly give birth to a *policy*, for a policy could only, in practice, be determined by the governments of nations. It was possible too that, one day, there might be a European Government but quite irresponsible (*dérisoire*) to act as if that day had come. So France had refused to let Europe get bogged down —and to get bogged down herself—in an artificial enterprise which would have emasculated the states, misled the peoples and prejudiced the independence of the Continent, and had proposed, in preference to it, a system of "co-operation." The German Government had accepted this idea in principle but it had been rejected by Italy and the Low Countries. It had also been attacked on the quite contradictory grounds (a) that it was non-federal, and (b) that it must include a non-federal Britain. Besides, Britain had conclusively demonstrated in "interminable" negotiations that she could not accept the economic rules of the EEC and further that her nuclear power could not be European as having no independence in relation to America.

This was why the Franco-German Treaty had been signed, in order to make a start. But though it had been useful from the point of view of establishing contacts it had not resulted in any common line of conduct, notably as regards defence, a new organization of the Atlantic Alliance, East/West relations, the frontiers of Eastern and Central Europe, the recognition of China, Viet Nam, Indonesia, aid to under-developed countries, or even the agricultural policy of the Six. The reason for this lamentable result was, simply, that Bonn had not, up to the present, made up its mind to have a policy that was European and independent. If this state of affairs persisted for long there was a risk that the French people would have doubts, and the German people anxieties, and that the others would mark time pending a dissolution of the whole affair. Nevertheless "the force of things" was achieving results—in spite of everything—and France at any rate was certain that she was "serving the balance, the peace and the progress of the universe."

What is rather fascinating about this obviously sincere, if egocentric, confession of faith is the one reference to "*L'Angleterre*." This country is clearly not included in Europe, since her population is not German, or Latin, or Gallic. Nor is she specifically mentioned as having taken part either in the War or in the subsequent happy "*redressement*." Her nuclear potential is likewise not mentioned, though in July 1964, Britain already had hydrogen bombs in quantity and a highly significant fleet of bombers, while France at that moment had no developed nuclear weapons at all. Britain, in fact, only comes on the scene as an embarrassing and unqualified sup-plicant, embarrassing because she is not really Euro-pean, unqualified because she is a mere satellite of America. From the point of view of "Europe," in fact, it would clearly be far better if she were under the sea. In any case, the best way to "*faire l'Europe*" is to pro-ceed as if she were not there.

The year closed with yet another invocation of the Franco-German Treaty (concluded under the auspices of Charlemagne) at Strasbourg; with a rare mention of Italy, "so dear to France and so necessary to Europe"; and with a short philippic against "integration" and "Atlanticism" to say nothing of "supra-nationalism," which now also appeared to be raising its ugly head. But in February 1965 there was, at a Press Conference in Paris, a considered and important statement regarding the German problem in its European context. After rehearsing the sad history of the German race, uncertainty about whose boundaries had often produced a sort of "*furor teutonicus*," the General recalled how the Cold War had resulted in the division of Germany; how the "roll-back" policy of John Foster Dulles could not work because the West was not prepared for war; how many people had become reconciled to this division; but how, owing to the uncertainty deriving from it, it could not last for ever. It could, however, only be ended by agreement between East and West, which meant by understanding between and joint action by all the peoples interested, namely the peoples of Europe.

This was the only way to maintain Europe in a state of balance, peace and co-operation from one end to another within the limits that nature had given her. Admittedly it would be a long time before the vast and complicated problem could be solved. Russia would have to evolve and liberate herself from her totalitarian regime, getting rather nearer to the free peoples of the West. Her satellites would have to play their due part in a reconstructed Europe. Germany, for her part, would have to agree on her frontiers and not have any armaments other than those agreed to by *all* her neighbours (my italics). The *Six* (my italics) would have to form a political organization in order to "achieve a new balance" on the Continent. And so Europe, "the mother of modern civilization," would establish herself "from the Atlantic to the Urals" in such a way as to fulfil, in conjunction with "America, her daughter," the role which was her due as regards "the progress of two milliard human beings who had such terrible need of it." This vision was followed by a short reference to the pleasure which the General had experienced at meeting the British Prime Minister during the funeral ceremonies of the *"grand Churchill"*—which was certainly genuine if the rumour is true that at that meeting Harold Wilson expressed admiration for de Gaulle and general agreement with his various policies.

Several inferences can be drawn from this remarkable statement. In the first place the European "balance" contemplated was clearly one between a Western Europe, led by France, and an Eastern Europe, presumably led by a new, and liberal Russia. In the second place, the construction was likely to take a very long time to achieve, and until it was achieved there would be no question of Britain's joining the French-led Western Europe. In the third place, although Germany might finish up by being reunified, this was nowhere explicitly stated. Reunified or not, she would nevertheless have to accept certain servitudes, notably as regards her armaments and her boundaries. In any case there would be no question of American troops remaining on the Continent, nor British troops either for that matter. France and Russia

—both nuclear powers, of course—would in some way control the centre of the Continent, and no doubt it was thought that France, by reason of her primacy, as it were, in civilization, would arrange for her policies and ideas to prevail over those of an only recently civilized Russia, and one, too, which had in some inexplicable way been separated from her Asian "Empire"—presumably by handing it over to China.

Strange as it may seem to some, this "vision" is almost certainly the real faith of the General. Just as Saint Joan had her "voices" so has he his: it is France which is always whispering in his ear. "This country," as he said a little later, "this France who has healed her wounds—God only knows how severe they were!—this France, which is regaining her power and her influence; this France who is more and more respected from one end of the world to the other, well, she is concerned with establishing among the peoples, whoever they may be, wherever they may be, and irrespective of their ideologies, their regimes, their divisions, the contacts necessary for creating in the world a balance, not that of Yalta ... but a new one based on the independence and responsibility of every single one of the nations of the earth." This herculean, this literally cosmic programme, once defined, was developed with mounting enthusiasm and eloquence in speech after speech during the earlier part of 1965 which saw—as de Gaulle several times pointed out— several great physical achievements designed to link the centre of Europe with its neighbours, namely the canalization of the Moselle, the tunnel under Mont Blanc, and virtual agreement on the Channel Tunnel too. Developed, that is to say, until the crisis in the Common Market at the end of June to which we have already referred.[5]

After that the world had to wait two months before a very long pronouncement justifying the French withdrawal from Brussels and throwing most of the blame on to the European Commission. In this document it was also made clear, as we have already seen, that France would not accept the provision of the Treaty of Rome establishing the E E C whereby (after 1 January 1966) certain decisions would have to be taken by weighted majority voting. But the philosophy which led up to this conclusion did not vary, save, perhaps, that the case against federalism was even more vigorously put than usual. "According to these dreams," the General declared, "the countries concerned would lose their national personality." Further, "in the absence of a Federator in the West which, each in his own way, Charlemagne, Otto, Charles V, Napoleon and Hitler tried to be, and Stalin too, in the

[5] De Gaulle only seems to have lost his temper once during this "prophetic" period. That was when he was told by a journalist that the European policy of France was still not understood. He was tired of explaining, he said, that it was a question of a *confederation* and not a *fusion*, not something supra-national based on Strasbourg in which co-opted technocrats took crucial decisions in "their offices." It was easy to be a "Jean-foutre" (term of abuse). Then, when further pestered with enquiries whether, after all, the United States had not emerged from a "supra-national fusion" he said that was totally different. America was virgin country where the pioneers found only the bones of a few redskins that they had bumped off [*zigouillés*]. And anyhow it had been necessary to have a Civil War, which was still going on.

East," Europe would be run by that old and even more horrifying monster, a "technocratic non-national, irresponsible Areopagus" which would, though the General did not say why, inevitably come under the domination of America and be merged in the dreaded "Atlantic Community." It need hardly be said that, as against this unnatural conception, France proposed a Confederation which "one day" could admit countries such as Britain or Spain that, like France, could not agree to "lose their sovereignty." France, indeed, stood for national independence and, though no longer the "mastodon" that she was under Louis XIV, was well qualified to conduct Europe along this road. Qualified "because of her nature which inclined her towards human contacts. Qualified because of the historical opinion formed of her by reason of which she enjoyed a sort of latent credit when it was a question of universal things. Qualified because she had shed all the colonial holds which she used to have over other peoples. Qualified lastly because she was seen to be a nation with free hands whose policy was not influenced by any outside pressures." In short, because France was not like any other country, but enjoyed a special, not to say, a unique position in the world. The position was clearer than ever. If France's partners wanted her to return they must accept her leadership.

At the end of November, however, the General suddenly gave out that there were some indications that the conditions which had previously held up a "rapprochement" of Great Britain with Continental Europe were diminishing in importance. "The problem seemed to be slowly ripening in a positive sense." A springe to catch the woodcock of the pro-British Five? A gesture towards Edward Heath, who had just seen the General and might in a few months' time be Prime Minister? In the light of certain declarations just over two years later, either looks quite likely.

Meanwhile the only thing to do was to sit tight and hope that the Five would give in—and the date of the Presidential Election was fast approaching. There is little doubt that the failure of the General to obtain in the first round a clear majority of votes in that election was the fear, particularly evident among the farmers, that he might be preparing to break up the Common Market. Before the second ballot, therefore, de Gaulle staged two masterly television interviews with Michel Droit. The first was largely devoted to France, her unique role, and the duty of the French to support France. The second was an answer to certain very direct questions such as: "Are you trying to torpedo the Common Market on the agricultural issue?" "Is it not true that a 'Europe des Patries' is not enough and a 'Europe from the Atlantic to the Urals' much too much of a good thing?" "Are you really a 'European' at all?"

First of all, the General very reasonably stressed the necessity of free competition in a larger market as a condition for progress. Then he recalled his victory in winning over Germany to accept free trade in foodstuffs in 1963. But he next accused his partners of not abiding by their pledge to get agreement on the financing of the agreed agricultural settlement of 30 January, and in trying to get France to accept unacceptable "political conditions," in plain English, to abide by the terms of the Treaty of Rome. "Solidarity" between Western nations should indeed be achieved, but nations could not help remaining nations and you could not make Europe by jumping up and down in your chair and shouting "Europe." Thus, politically speaking, you could only have "co-operation" and, in seeking this, reconcile national policies and interests, which were naturally not always the same.

France had proposed precisely this ever since 1961. In an attempt to go a little further she had also concluded an actual Treaty with Germany, though that had not as yet had many results. But when people shouted "supra-nationality that is the only thing" they were talking through their hats. It was attractive enough to think in terms of myths and chimaeras, but they remained chimaeras and myths. No, the only practical thing to do was to get back to 1961 and when France had surmounted the present crisis—which he believed she would do—it was "very probable that, a little earlier, a little later," Britain would join us, and that would be quite natural. But she would not join a supra-national Europe. It would be a Europe acting by co-operation between States. Later, this might well become a Confederation. He did not exclude that possibility at all.

Though it obviously did not give him full satisfaction the subsequent Luxemburg "Compromise" of 30 January 1966, was hailed by de Gaulle as a "great and happy event." For the first time since the beginnings of the Common Market it had been possible to depart from the "kind of fiction" whereby the economic organization of Europe ought to stem from some centre other than that of the States, with their powers and responsibilities. Reason had now prevailed and there was no longer any danger of a "usurpation of sovereignty" either by the exercise of majority voting or by an undue extension of the powers of the Commission. But, that being so, it was obviously necessary to proceed with political co-operation.

In any case the General felt much stronger and better able to follow his own policy, whether or not he could get his partners to "co-operate" in pursuit of France's national aims. Without informing them of his intention he announced on 7 March that France was leaving NATO. A little later it was announced that he was visiting the Soviet Union. Perhaps the unfortunate Dr Erhard had received advance notification of this last important step; but he was on the way out. In December the "Great Coalition" was to come into operation. Convinced, apparently, by the General's eloquence, the German Gaullists were preparing to take over the direction of German foreign policy. Was there real hope for the Plan after all?

5

Success in Sight? (1966-68)

FROM HIS Caravelle high over Germany, the President, on his way to Moscow, addressed a telegram to his colleague and special ally, President Lübke. His thoughts, he said, went out to his colleague and to the German people "which had its important place in a Europe restored to its vocation of balance and of peace." An hour or two later, on arrival at Vnukovo Airport, he told the President of the USSR that "We know, you and I, as the USSR and France know, as Europe knows, as the Universe knows, what importance attaches to the visit which I have the honour to pay you. For the object of the two countries, among others, is to exchange their views, and, I hope, concert their actions in order to foster the security of the Continent as well as the balance, the progress and the peace of the entire world."

These quotations bring out the difficulty that besets the mediator. What, indeed, would be the "important place" reserved for a reunited Germany? And how, if this "place" was to be acceptable to Russia, which had suffered so appallingly at the hands of the old Great German Reich, was it likely to appeal to the present German people? On the same night of his arrival in Moscow the General advanced, in public before his Russian hosts his own preliminary ideas. "Peaceful coexistence" was good, so far as it went, but it did not go far enough. It was in any case vitiated by the Vietnamese War. France, for her part, rejected the "rigid confrontation" of the two Super-Powers and, while remaining a member of the Atlantic Alliance and a "free and Western nation," would like to break "the evil spell" which had so far prevented the establishment of "new relationships" between herself and "the European States said to be Eastern" leading to "detente, entente and co-operation."

In the first instance such "new relationships" should be established with the USSR because Russia was "much the greatest power in her region." Besides, France saw in Russia a partner with whom collaboration was "entirely natural." No fundamental quarrel separated them, and never had, not even during the Napoleonic and Crimean Wars. Thus the war alliance was a natural thing and so "in order that the international situation should develop in accordance with good sense, Paris had necessarily to address herself to Moscow." Without underestimating the part played by the United States of America it was, for France, the re-establishment of Europe that was the supreme issue. An "entente" between states hitherto antagonists was a *European* problem, and it was this principle that should be applied to the German problem. "While awaiting the day, however, when the whole of Europe could concert on ways and means of achieving this end, everything suggested that France and the Soviet Union should go ahead together at the present time." In other words, he appeared to make a direct appeal to Russia to come forward with a plan for a German settlement jointly agreed with France over the head of America.

This was something to which the Russians, however delighted they may have been by the General's action in disrupting NATO, in weakening the Western Alliance, and in leading a world-wide anti-American crusade, could not accept. If they had, they would have ruined all prospect of a real detente with the United States and not secured a German settlement either. For the only kind of German solution to which they could, within a generation of the mass murders in the Ukraine, agree would have been one which would inevitably have been turned down by the government at Bonn. They proceeded therefore to parade their guest over great tracts of the USSR and to flatter him to the limit of their power. For them, he was undoubtedly a very valuable asset.

During his triumphal tour, de Gaulle naturally visited some of the capitals of the huge Union and at one point found himself flying over the famous "chain of the mountains of the Urals" which he had for so long hailed as the Eastern limit of "Europe." Probably to his astonishment, the mountains could not be seen. The Great Russian plain, covered with forests, slowly rose two or three thousand feet to a watershed not distinguishable from the air. To the East the forests rolled on interminably through Siberia, which contained something like thirty million Great Russians in no way dissimilar from those to the West of the continental dividing line. Novosibirsk was found to be a completely Russian town. It was clear that, economically, politically, culturally, the Urals were no barrier. Only geographically could they be said to provide a limit, and even geographically it was no longer evident why. No longer evident, it would seem, to the General himself, who, on leaving Russia, only drank a health to Europe "from one end to the other," and it did not look as if even that was going to develop in accordance with his dream. So at this point we ought to try to discover why it was that for years General de Gaulle had employed the phrase "Europe from the Atlantic to the Urals" (or its equivalent) to describe the very basis, the apparent quintessence, of his "vast plan."

Let us begin by forgetting about the Urals. He was, presumably, misled by Larousse into thinking that Siberia—part, in his imagination, of the Russian Empire—could be separated from Russia in a way that, nationally considered, might be just conceivable in the case of, for instance, Georgia, Latvia or Uzbekistan. As we have already noticed, the scheme, however exactly defined, was for the creation of a "wider Europe" which would include the Great Russians, the Ukrainians and all the subject peoples between the Elbe and the Curzon Line,[1] the EEC, the continental members of EFTA, together with Spain, but not the United States or (for a very long time at any rate) the United Kingdom. In this "wider Europe" the two German states would somehow be reunified or anyhow confederated, but would be subjected to certain agreed rules or "servitudes" which would prevent them from becoming once again a menace to their neighbours. The Germans would, however, apparently have some say in policy making, as would all the other participants—some 36 if the proposal is to be taken literally—though the major decisions would no doubt be taken jointly by France, the leader of Western, and Soviet Russia, the leader of Eastern, Europe. At least it must be assumed that this would be the substance of the plan, since short of a Federation—to which the General has always been violently opposed—there is hardly any other basis on which the proposed new system could function as any sort of entity. And if it is not conceived of as some sort of entity, then what, in practice, can it really be intended to be?

[1] The Eastern, or ethnic frontier of Poland.

The faithful and intelligent Couve de Murville who —usually unaware of them in advance—had for almost ten years the exacting task of rationalizing a number of the more sybilline pronouncements of his Chief, has had a go. On 4 February 1963, the Minister told the Foreign Affairs Commission of the Senate that "Europe from the Atlantic to the Urals is not a topical project. It is associated with the idea that, in the ultimate analysis, a real European settlement will be necessary, and that a Europe will be discovered which has its own balance. The long-term objective of a union of all Europe should be stated in relation to the evolution of Russia, which has been great since Stalin. But, for the moment, one can only note the fact that the USSR does not seek an agreement with Europe of the Six, and is not disposed to enter into a dialogue with anybody other than the United States." This is all very well but what exactly *is* the object of the whole exercise? "Detente, entente, co-operation" is the General's formula. Detente seems to suggest the beginning of a German settlement. American forces presumably begin to leave Europe: possibly there is a corresponding reduction in the Soviet Army in East Germany. The main lines of the settlement emerge. We consequently arrive at the entente. What happens then? Who copes with the huge difficulties connected with the supervision of Germany or the Germans? In the first instance, France and Russia, presumably, who will have to "co-operate" for that purpose. But if they are to do so there must be a machine, for, after all, the other 34 states must also be able at least to record their point of view. And if there is a machine—in Vienna, in Berlin?—then it is going to be very difficult to get agreement if, as would be inevitable under the General's theory, the unanimity rule prevails.

What is likely to happen if the Russians turn up one day and suggest that United Europe should approve the action they have taken to appropriate the bulk of the oil of the Persian Gulf? Or demand that recognition should be given to some revolutionary government in Latin America? It might be easier if the idea simply was that each of the major European powers—France and Russia—should confer first with their own satellites and then try to reach agreement between themselves. Only, if that were so, it is difficult to see how, in such a dialogue, the advantage would not inevitably rest with the Soviet Union. In other words, if the scheme were ever put into effective operation, the only certain loser would be likely to be France.

There are, therefore, those who maintain that the entire conception is simply advanced for tactical purposes and is not seriously meant. We shall discuss this theory subsequently but I may say here and now that if the General does not believe in the possible formation of his "wider" Europe, he is an even greater actor than I think he is. It may be that this dream of "Europe" is, essentially, not a dream which he expects to come true in any physical sense; but that he regards it as a sort of formula, as a sort of imaginary structure in accordance with which it is possible to arrange for an ever-greater role for France is, I believe, certain. And no doubt de Gaulle sincerely believes that this process would be in the long-term interests of "Europe," however defined, and the world. What is rather extraordinary, however, is that he should think that the Great Russian nation is more "European" than America—"Europe's daughter" as we have already heard him say. The idea that Western Europe, which for the last 600 years has looked towards the Ocean should suddenly feel greater sympathy for the rather alien lands of Eastern Europe beyond the Curzon Line than for the New World is paradoxical. These lands (with the exception of the Baltic States) Christianized from Byzantium only in the tenth century, and subsequently largely dominated by Tartars and Turks, have always had a different approach to life from that of the Western and Central European countries, as indeed can now be seen in the fundamental differences of outlook between the Russians and their minor European "allies." Even if the Russians suddenly became "liberal"—and why should they, since throughout their history this great people have always preferred to have a dictatorial regime— the concept of a "Region" extending from Gibraltar to Vladivostok (or at any rate to Omsk) hardly makes sense. Even if it were ever formed, what would happen to the General's "balance"? Who would be balanced against whom?

It is indeed possible to imagine a Western Europe —comprising all the Western European democracies, for otherwise it would not be strong enough—in some kind of "special relationship" with certain Central European states, holding a kind of balance between America and Russia. But for such a "balance" to be formed there would have to be an Authority of some kind in Western Europe. It is inconceivable, in fact, that Western Europe, or one day an even wider Europe could emerge in any other circumstances. Since the General would not allow this to happen, and

since he would not admit other fully qualified European
states to membership of the only Community which
at present exists, it is not easy to understand how he
expected ever to achieve his "balance." What is certain
is that he was not able to explain the theory satisfactorily to the Russians; for the communiqué issued
at the end of his 1966 visit scarcely corresponded to
the tremendous possibilities conjured up on the first
evening after his arrival. It was agreed that "detente"
was a good thing and that "the problems of Europe
should first of all be discussed within the limits of
Europe" but that was really all. Besides, it was apparently admitted that the European settlement, if it were
ever negotiated, would have to be guaranteed by
America as well as by Russia. But, if so, then surely
the United States of America would have to be in the
negotiations from the start; they could not be conducted by France and the USSR alone. And what
about Britain, whose forces would still presumably,
be present in West Berlin?

It was therefore not unnatural that de Gaulle should
once again turn to the Germans who, no doubt expect-
ing a rebuff, had been very understanding as regards
his Russian venture. The trouble about the Germans
and the French, he said, in Bonn, on 21 July, was that
they were "too reticent": they should therefore confide in each other more and things would go better.
"Detente, entente, co-operation" was still, however,
the slogan necessary for "the whole of Europe" in
which Germany "as a whole" had, evidently, a great
part to play. Indeed, the one goes with the other—
"Europe as a whole, Germany as a whole." It was with
this objective in mind that he had visited recently

"the Eastern part of our Continent." This was not with any intention of repudiating or trampling upon "our Atlantic Alliance or our friendships, though both ought of necessity to be adapted to changed conditions." Well said: but it is permissible to wonder what would have been said if by any chance the Russians had given the green light to his original suggestions.

Back in Paris, the General, as was his custom, summed up the situation at a Press Conference on 28 October. Apart from the Communists, who still indulged in the dream of the International, three groups wanted France to allow her policy to be determined in a "Europe" ready-made for this purpose, her defence in NATO, her monetary policy in Washington, her "personality" in the United Nations. They were the supra-nationalists; those who feared the East and thought that France's interests were bound up with the "Atlantic West"; and those who put their faith in "the supreme advantage of some universal arbiter." But acceptance by France of any of these courses of action would have ended up in her acceptance of American hegemony. If that ever happened, France would disappear, "borne off by the chimaeras." His own (opposite) policy of independence had not led to the predicted disasters and in his view France's proposals regarding Viet Nam, NATO, and the international monetary problems, would be advantageous for everybody, even for the United States. His formula, too, of "detente, entente and co-operation" was perfectly compatible with good Franco-German relations. It was, indeed, lamentable that the Franco-German Treaty had not produced better results, but, after all, Franco-German relations were at least cordial, and it had now been agreed that French troops would stay on in Germany—at no cost, incidentally, to the German tax-payer. Meanwhile, the Common Market had been "saved" by the French veto on British entry in 1963 and by the French unilateral action in 1965. This last action had been particularly salutary, in that it had led, in 1966, to final agreement on Agriculture.

Yet political co-operation was still necessary! Always France had proposed this on one condition: that her partners should contemplate and follow a policy which was European. This was the condition which had prevented its accomplishment up till now. But even if it did come about "nothing of any lasting value would emerge until such time as the peoples of the West and the peoples of the East had come together." Certainly no reunification of Germany would be conceivable save in this setting. But what a prospect it would be! Already the results of his visit to Russia were becoming known—economic, cultural, scientific and technical. France was "renewing, positively and profoundly, her relations with the Eastern European States." The Cold War was "no longer serious." It was in such circumstances that France was going ahead with her nuclear programme and by 1970 would be the proud possessor of a hydrogen bomb. "Tearing ourselves away from the myths of renunciation which kept our country in a state of subordination, we have established our national independence as regards foreign policy and defence, in which sphere we provide ourselves with all the means necessary to deter aggression on the part of any other power." It is towards the end of 1966, in fact, that we first hear the formulation of a new French defence policy which has an important bearing on French European policy and should therefore now be analysed separately in some detail.

We have seen how in March 1958 the Fourth Republic decided to proceed with the manufacture of an atomic bomb. There were few who would blame the French for embarking on such a venture, for which the post-war Labour Government of Clement Attlee had set an example. France was, after all, one of the Five Permanent Members of the Security Council; she had special responsibilities conferred on her by the Charter of the United Nations; she was still, in early 1958, at the head of a "Community" which embraced large parts of Africa and outlying districts in other parts of the globe. It was quite arguable, too, that the "spin-off" from a military nuclear programme would have very considerable economic advantages. But, above all, perhaps, was the feeling that if the United Kingdom had a nuclear potential, why should not France have one too? The "special relationship" with America which Britain was supposed to possess was also a powerful motive, though as a matter of fact, as regards nuclear matters, it only became a reality with the second amendment of the McMahon Act in June 1958, that is to say a month after General de Gaulle came into power.

In any case the decision to go ahead was inspired by much the same motives that inspired the British Government to do the same thing in 1946 after President Truman had refused to continue the Anglo-American joint programme or to give any information to the British to enable them to proceed with theirs.

And in both cases the eventual result was to place before both countries a terrible choice, which of course first confronted the British, who had started ten or twelve years earlier. This was, what exactly does a medium-sized power do with nuclear weapons once she has got them, and how is she, short of crippling expenditure, to prevent them from getting out of date, when most of the vast outlay will, presumably, have been wasted?

At the end of 1968, the French Government, after the expenditure, according to George Ball,[2] over some ten years of around $15,000 million, or, at the old parity, about £600 million a year, has only just succeeded in exploding a thermonuclear bomb. But she had now commissioned a force of some 40 excellent supersonic Mirage IV nuclear bombers (which would have to be refuelled from the air before they arrived at their destination, if they ever did). Few believe that this force, which could probably anyhow be destroyed on the ground by a few unheralded Soviet medium-range ballistic missiles, is likely to be "credible," as the saying goes, from the point of view of the United States or the Soviet Union, whatever its effect may be on the Germans, or other European countries. By 1970–71, however, France expects to have some 27 intermediate-range ground-to-ground ballistic missiles (IRBMs) installed in hardened silos in the Vaucluse, each with war-heads yielding 120–180 kilotons.

It may take a year or two longer to install this system in its entirety, but when and if it is installed it could undoubtedly have some "deterrent" value,

[2] *The Discipline of Power*, Bodley Head, 1967.

though by (say) 1975 it seems likely that not very many of these missiles would reach their target, given the probable perfecting by that time of the Russian anti-ballistic-missile system which should be able to cope with all but multiple-head missiles in large quantities. But by the middle seventies France should have, in addition, two or three nuclear submarines, each with 16 IRBMs. The existence of such a fleet (which we must, on past form, presume) will certainly help to make France "credible" as a nuclear power; but even when it is fully operational the French will still not be much further on than the British with their four (or five) nuclear submarines armed with Polaris missiles. The question would be for them, as it is now for us, to what political use can we put our small nuclear potential? If it cannot be taken seriously by either of the Super-Powers, why is it necessary to spend money on it at all? And how can it be taken seriously when its use, even in a desperate emergency, could hardly be resorted to, seeing that, if it were, France and Britain would literally cease to exist, while the damage to the Super-Power concerned, even if grave, would certainly not be mortal? In other words, the bluff would, inevitably, be called.

However, a further possibility was looming on the French horizon at the end of 1966. That was to proceed eventually to a final stage, namely the construction of intercontinental ballistic missiles (ICBMs) with several times the range and perhaps the power of the IRBMs now being installed in Provence, coupled with a considerable extension of the nuclear submarine fleet. By this means, France would, in theory, be able to throw her weight about in all parts, or almost all parts of the world. In shorthand, it is called the policy of "*tous azimuts*" or all points of the compass. If such a system was installed round about 1980 it might indeed give more "credibility" to France's nuclear potential, though the cost would be tremendous and very probably crippling. It would therefore only seem to make any kind of sense if it formed a part of a joint European (or Western European) effort, involving a similar development of the British nuclear force, plus, no doubt, some assistance from the Germans as well. Is such a thing conceivable? If so, is it desirable? And would it ever be acceptable to General de Gaulle? This is indeed a question of relevance to the European policy of any nationalistic French Government.

It seems probable that the General for his part would prefer his own kind of Europe—his French-led "Confederation"—to rely on an enlarged French deterrent, provided only that his partners were persuaded to contribute handsomely to it. He has never, in any case, departed from his principle that the Germans, divided or reunited, should in no circumstances have anything to do with the manufacture or deployment of nuclear weapons. And as for the British nuclear potential, this he has usually ignored, though he has, in private, as I have some reason to believe, hinted that we should be most ill-advised to abandon it. What seems quite impossible, given his general attitude towards "Europe" which we have described at some length already, is that he should contemplate (*a*) any collective direction of a European Nuclear Force, or (*b*) any suggestion that such a Force should in any way form part—even as an autonomous unit—of some enduring Western alliance. The furthest he could possibly be induced to go would be to accept some liaison on targeting, between the British and French nuclear Forces. If it were ever formed, therefore, a European Force would have to be at the disposal of a "Europe" entirely independent of either Super-Power, and thus able, in accordance with de Gaulle's original thought, to throw its weight now on the side of one, and now on the side of the other. All this amounts to saying that if the crucial nuclear issue is to be solved in a European context, it can, under de Gaulle's theory, only be solved if Europe becomes the equivalent of a Super-Power under the general direction of France. If Britain will not accept such a solution, then she can either be isolated or join America. It should also be noted that, even if nuclear strength itself were built up to Super-Power standards it would still not be accompanied by any credible anti-ballistic-missile system.

Nor does the theory that a comparatively small French nuclear force would have the possibility of "triggering off" American nuclear action or threat of action hold water. Supposing that there was some incident involving the European allies of the United States which the United States preferred to meet by "conventional" means or not to meet at all, is it conceivable that threatened nuclear action by France against the Soviet Union would necessarily involve the nuclear power of America? Once again, all that would happen in such an event would be that the French bluff would be called. In the wise words of Mr Wolf-Mendl "There is no serious evidence that the Soviet Union has ceased to regard the United

States of America as the real partner when dealing
with major world problems." But even if, *per impos-
sibile*, France were to "replace the United States of
America as Russia's partner in the dialogue over Germany, a situation may arise in which the vital interests of France clash with those of Russia. . . . This
would lead to precisely that kind of confrontation
which the French regard as inadmissible"[3]—inadmissible, indeed, for at that moment they would be down
the drain. Or to quote the shrewd judgment of
Alastair Buchan, "It seems to be doubtful that the
French public really wishes to pay the price for a
'*tous azimuts*' strategy, or that such a strategy would
survive de Gaulle, even if he manages to whip it over
the parliamentary hurdles for the next few years. Perhaps the greatest interest . . . is his conception of the
world of the future, one in which there is no European
Political Community or even co-operation; in which a
large number of nuclear powers pursue an unbridled
Weltpolitik in a world of chaos; in which alliances
are picked up and dropped as occasion serves on the
Ribbentrop-Molotov pattern; and in which states retain no flexibility below the level of nuclear threats
for the protection of their interests; a world which
makes Orwell sound like Pollyanna."[4] Whatever may
be thought of this judgment it must surely be admitted that the pursuit of this policy is not consistent
with the pursuit of plans for European unity that can
be defined in any realistic terms.

However, it was towards the end of 1966, when
this policy was beginning to be formulated; when the
General was starting to bear the dollar in a big way

[3] *The World Today.*   [4] *Interplay*, May 1968.

and to infuriate the Americans by accumulating as much gold as he could; when it had become clear that, in the eyes of Moscow, at any rate, he was still not an *interlocuteur valable*; when for nearly four years he had been repeating, at intervals, that the kind of "Europe" which he favoured was not one which included the United Kingdom, anyhow for a long period of time, that two things happened: the Germans installed a new Government that proposed to apply a new "*Ostpolitik*" seeming to depend largely for its success on the assistance of the French Government, and the British leadership, largely under the influence of George Brown the then Minister for Economic Affairs, decided to have another shot at entering the Common Market. The first undoubtedly encouraged the General to pursue his Plan for a "*détente à la française*": the second was regarded by him as a serious challenge which it was essential to meet. For with Britain once in the Community how could he possibly proceed with his "war of movement" designed, above all, to keep France in the lead? And, in addition, before he had succeeded in getting the Americans out of Germany, Britain in the EEC could only represent a "Trojan Horse". Alfred Grosser says that the truth was that the General mistook his horse—it was German, not British! But M. Grosser was writing before the formation of the Great Coalition. New prospects were now opening up and de Gaulle's theories seemed to be becoming less unacceptable as time went on— as was natural since he had never had the slightest doubt of their basic validity. His allies, and indeed his adversaries (if, indeed, they were distinguishable) seemed to be gradually seeing the light.

6

The Plan Collapses (1968)

ON 10 MAY 1967, the British Labour Government
applied formally, under Article 237 of the Treaty of
Rome, for membership of the European Economic
Community, in the hope that at least negotiations
for entry would follow, it being the opinion of all
qualified jurists that a refusal on the part of the Six
even to negotiate would be a clear breach of that
Article of the Treaty. They had come round almost
full circle from the attitude they adopted at the end
of 1964 when they assumed power with a very small
majority. Then it was a question rather of organizing
the Commonwealth and, above all, of cultivating the
British "special relationship" with the United States
of America. Disillusionment with the Commonwealth
spread rapidly in 1965; the "special relationship" with
America did not turn out to be so special after all;
and hard economic facts and a study of the dossiers
pointed in only one direction. After the following
elections in March 1966, when the majority was
greatly increased, the "Europeans" in the Cabinet
gradually got the upper hand. Towards the end of
that year the die was cast. If they possibly could, they
were "going into Europe."

The ground for the action had been carefully prepared, in the sense that the Government had made
known their intention long in advance; had obtained
the views of all the governments concerned in the
early part of 1967 by personal visits of the Prime
Minister and Foreign Secretary to the various capitals
as well as to the headquarters of the Community in
Brussels; and had actually had their proposed application, together with the few major outstanding points
which they maintained should be the subject of

negotiation with the Six, approved by the House of Commons by one of the largest majorities ever known. They must therefore have had some reasons for thinking that their application would be successful within a fairly short period, after which any remaining difficulties could be smoothed out by discussions within the group itself—obviously the most sensible outcome from everybody's point of view. At the very least, they may have thought it possible during long-drawn-out negotiations to narrow down the main outstanding difficulties in the way of British entry to the point at which it would no longer be practical politics for de Gaulle to go on refusing his consent, if that, indeed, was his intention. It can be argued that the British Government always thought that the General would probably veto their application but nevertheless went ahead with it (a) because they genuinely believed it was the right thing to do, (b) because if negotiations were once started there was a probability that they would be successful in the long run and (c) because if the General vetoed negotiations he would be shown up as opposed to British entry for purely political reasons. But no doubt they did think that they had a considerable chance of getting what they wanted.

So let us see, first, whether de Gaulle gave any indication that he was willing at least to contemplate the possibility of British entry. There had already been one veto, and from the many extracts we have given of his apparent views on how "Europe" should be formed it is clear that it was on political rather than on economic grounds that he most objected to British membership of the Community. Certainly there had been no indication in more recent public utterances that he had in any way changed his mind. Indeed, as late as 29 October 1966 he had spoken of how his 1963 veto had "saved the Common Market from wandering down a road that led nowhere." In December George Brown (by then Foreign Secretary) had an hour's talk with him at the Elysée, but there is no record of the General's saying that his attitude towards British entry had in any way weakened. Only a few days later the French Government tried to prevent the subject of the possible entry of the United Kingdom into the EEC even being discussed at a lunch organized in Brussels by the Dutch Foreign Minister. Finally during the official visit to Paris on 25 January of the Prime Minister, and the Secretary of State, it was evident from Couve de Murville's guarded statement, that no green light had been given to a possible British application.

It is quite true that immediately *after* the application in May 1967, the General made some appreciative remarks of the progress made in Britain of the European idea and said that "it could not be, and has never been a question of a veto," but he went on to throw buckets of cold water on the notion that Britain could, for various reasons, actually join the Community, even producing his old bugbear that if Britain and the other applicants joined the EEC it would inevitably become a sort of Free Trade Area which would, equally inevitably, come under the domination of the United States. What seems to be established is that at no time, and in no conversation with any British representative, did the General let it be supposed that he was in favour of Britain's joining the EEC—at any rate for a long period. Nor had any change been got out of the visit of Prime Minister Pompidou and Foreign Minister Couve de Murville to London in July 1966—rather the reverse. It was merely a study in mutual incomprehension. In any case neither of the guests, future leaders of France though they probably both are, had the last word in the formulation of French foreign policy. Therefore it must have been the calculation of the British Government (a) that de Gaulle would not be able to hold up negotiations and (b) that once they started he would be unable in the long run to resist pressure from his partners (all known to be favourable in principle to British entry) and notably from his German partner. What evidence, therefore, is there that the Germans, for their part, gave any indication of eventual action in this sense? There does not seem to be much.

The truth was that the new German government which had come into power on 1 December 1966— the "Great Coalition" of Christian Democrats and Socialists—feeling that "confrontation," membership of NATO, correct behaviour in the Council of Europe, WEU and so on had really got them nowhere so far as reunification was concerned, had made up its mind to pursue a different foreign policy, even if cautiously to start off with. The chief feature of this was to try to produce a "detente" in Central Europe which would further their ultimate aim, if not of actual physical reunification, at any rate of some new deal whereby both Western and Eastern parts of Germany might form part of a "wider" Europe— involving, conceivably, some form of association of the West with the Soviet Satellites. Naturally, the pursuit of this policy would begin simply with approaches to the Soviet satellite states for better relations, both political and economic, by no means excluding the German Democratic Republic. In the application of this new *Ostpolitik* they believed that General de Gaulle could be of great use to them as a kind of go-between with the East generally, even though they could not share his views on the desirability of dispensing with American protection and trusting to that provided by the Franco-German Treaty instead. They wanted, indeed, like so many people, to have it both ways: but for so long as they did they were not, if they could possibly help it, going to quarrel with General de Gaulle.

True, they were keen, on the whole, on Britain's joining the EEC and quite willing to intervene with the General in this sense; but Chancellor Kiesinger made it clear from the start that he was not going to apply pressure on the French. In the statement put out after his visit to London at the end of October 1967, that is to say when it had no doubt been represented to him strongly that he ought to do something about the General's increasingly intransigent attitude, he would only say that the Federal Government believed that Britain should be a member of the European Communities and that the German Government would "try to help overcome the difficulties that had arisen," trusting that negotiations would soon begin.

Fearing that the initiative might run into the sands, I had myself suggested, towards the end of 1966, that the Government might be well advised to go through all the preliminary hoops, including obtaining the approval of the House of Commons, and then inform the Six of their action, enquiring at the same time whether their attitude as explained in, and approved by Parliament, was a sufficient basis for negotiations on an application for formal membership made under Article 237 of the Treaty of Rome. In this way, I felt, the ball would be put into the opposing court; there would have been no loss of face implicit in a direct veto; and it might even have been more difficult for the Six to have refused to negotiate. Indeed any reply which they might have sent to a reasoned memorandum—perhaps constructed on the lines of Mr Brown's admirable speech to Western European Union on 4 July 1967—would in itself have been a form of negotiation. However, the Government did not accept this advice.

Later, after the application, I advanced the idea of a "delayed entry" whereby we should agree to sign the Treaty after broad agreement on one or two outstanding issues but not to become full members during a transitional period in which we should put our economy straight, discover the correct (perhaps a European) role for sterling and deal with the hundred and one decisions necessary before our economy and that of the Six could effectively be harmonized. Under this scheme we should have had observers on the Commission, with a right to be consulted on major changes of policy and should also have had (subject to certain reasonable safeguards for the Six) a certainty of eventual entry. In general, the scheme was not wholly unlike the one produced later by the intelligent and pro-British Valéry Giscard d'Estaing. But it was most unpopular with the Government, who appeared to think that it was a form of association (which it was not), and the "charge" continued to its rather predictable end in December 1967 when the General made it clear that he would not open negotiations and applied what is now known as the "Second Veto." And yet this time there was a difference.

It was different because this time there was no concealing the fact that the General's objection to British entry was entirely political, and connected solely with his determination to form "Europe" on the basis of a French-led non-supra-national "Confederation" which could not be maintained, as such, if it embraced Great Britain, any more, for that matter, than it could continue to exist in the event of any kind of German reunification. The simple fact that the detested Brussels Commission had reported that, in spite of admitted economic and financial difficulties, negotiations for British entry should certainly be begun, as well as the fact that this was the evident wish of France's five partners, made it abundantly clear that the French attitude was entirely arbitrary. As with the Caesars, Reason had been subordinated to Will—*Sic volo sic jubeo sit pro ratione voluntas*.

The elaborate defence of his veto which the President made at a Press Conference on 27 November 1967 was, indeed, about as feeble in argument as can be imagined. It consisted in repeating that the British would have to "subject themselves to fundamental changes ... necessary for the country to settle in its own equilibrium"—whatever that might mean. "A radical transformation" was also necessary "to enable her to join the Continentals. This is obvious from the political point of view." Needless to say, there was no indication as to what changes would be necessary. The rest was a series of derogatory remarks about the weakness of the British economy and currency, how different, he said, from the "solid, interdependent and assured society in which the Franc, the Mark, the Lira, the Belgian Franc and the Florin are brought together." A Franc that was "solid and assured?" Well, well. But it must have been evident to all that the only reason for Britain's exclusion was because his own personal policy could no longer be pursued if she were a member. The Prime Minister's excellent point-by-point refutation was hardly needed.

It was different this time because the Kiesinger government was not having much success with its *Ostpolitik*, more particularly with its new approach to the DDR which had replied by making things even more difficult in Berlin. Besides, the tremendous efforts of the General to induce the Poles and the Rumanians to detach themselves from the Eastern *bloc* were not meeting with much success either. Whatever their views on independence, the satellites remained highly suspicious of German reunification and were certainly not prepared for any major break with the Soviet Union. If they thought that there was some real chance of entering into a new relationship, economic no doubt, to start off with, with a Western Europe which accepted the fact of the continued existence of two German States and which was not out for any kind of domination, merely proposing more mutually advantageous trade, then they might be attracted—to the extent that Big Brother would let them. But this situation can only come about when Western Europe is really formed, together with Britain and the other applicants, and the attempt to transform it into a pale imitation of the First French Empire has been finally abandoned.

It is true that for so long as the French think that by pretending to encourage the Germans while maintaining good relations with the Russians, they can avoid the Germans taking over the Common Market, and so long as the Germans think that, by flattering the French, this is exactly what they will be able to do in the long run, little progress will be made towards the constitution of a valid "Europe." But when both realize that such dreams are not very likely to appeal to the Super-Powers they will no doubt both return to earth and consider policies that are realistic and practical. For there is no doubt at all that a Western Europe which included Britain, but not otherwise, could, if it spoke as one voice, have sufficient strength to make that voice heard in the dialogue of the Great and hence to ensure a better and less hazardous future for our Continent, and indeed for all mankind.

Different, too, because the shock the second veto produced on the British people was less than that produced by the first. Then they had thought that it was only a question of making up their collective mind; now they realized that they had an active adversary in their way. Let us hope that this seeming reverse will encourage them in their determination to join the Community, for to be virtually ordered by a French President to go off and join America was at least a challenge. It certainly does not look as if they would be particularly keen on "co-operating" with the Six on major projects while they are still excluded from the Common Market. If we had come in it is obvious that ELDO, for instance, would still be a going concern, and that common ventures in the aeronautics industry would be much less uncertain than they now are. As J.-J. Servan-Schreiber points out in his recent powerful book,[1] the French ought to realize that unless France really wants to become an industrial satellite of America her only hope is to patch things up with *L'Angleterre* who, Servan-Schreiber says, is clearly, from this angle, France's best friend and natural ally. It is quite possible that this simple reflection may soon occur to many in the vast, disparate majority in the French National Assembly, still, theoretically, at the disposal of a French President. Let us hope so. It is later than we think.

Different, finally, because the events of May 1968 showed that all was not well with the Gaullist system. After the first veto France went from strength to strength. For that matter Britain, contrary to some gloomy predictions, did not do so badly either. But five months after the second veto, France lost £1,000 million in two months; billions of francs were pouring over the Swiss frontier; the regime was tottering; and for a week hardly a Gaullist was to be found in Paris. It would be absurd to say that the veto had anything to do with these distressing events, or indeed with the subsequent rally and victory of the *bien pensants*. But what the events did seem to show was that the basic nationalistic philosophy of General de Gaulle was somehow inadequate, inadequate in any case for the bulk of the younger generation, some half a million of whom could not be registered and thus failed to vote. Something new was evidently required in France. Is it

[1] *Le Défi Americain*, Denoel, 1967.

too much to hope that the French will once again turn their thoughts from *grandeur* to "Europe"? Why should they not, when the rape of Czechoslovakia destroyed the whole basis of the General's European policy, namely "detente, entente and co-operation with the Russians," in other words, the formation of "Europe" with the Soviet Government and without the United Kingdom?

After the *évènements* it did not look, in any case, as if the aged leader had much energy left to apply his "vast plan" which, as we have noted, entirely collapsed after the second *coup de Prague*. There were indeed mutterings in the French press that since the French position had been discovered to be so vulnerable there could be no question of even discussing the remote possibility of the entry of a potential competitor into the EDC. Too weak to enter in 1967, it may well be that Britain will be considered too strong to enter in 1970 or in 1971. Any argument will be good enough to exclude the British for so long as the French think in nationalistic terms only and not in the interests of the group as a whole. And yet there must be many Frenchmen who feel that, in this modern world, extreme nationalism is essentially irrational and, if pursued in Europe, can only lead to the total hegemony of one or the other of the Super-Powers. If there are such, it is to be hoped that they will come out clearly with criticisms of the European policy of any French Government dominated by Gaullist conceptions.

How many of them, I wonder, could now seriously sustain the thesis of their Chief as elaborated on 9 September 1968 in the funeral oration on his policy when he alleged that his real reason for excluding Britain from the Common Market was because if she came in, it would be dominated by the United States of America, as would, inevitably, any supra-national system? Why? Any rational student of the present situation must indeed now come to precisely the reverse conclusion: it is only by forming a supra-national Community with the United Kingdom that "Europe" has the slightest chance of avoiding domination by one or the other of the Super-Powers. Hopefully, the generality of the French may even have reached this conclusion before this book appears.

Meanwhile, it must be hoped that, this time, perhaps behind the scenes, some real effort will be made to achieve basic Franco-British understanding. If it were discovered that many non-governmental people in positions of authority on both sides of the Channel were disturbed by the implications of the present situation, that would at least be something. Plans for joint action for achieving certain limited objectives might then be made. Short *colloques* (invitations to which tend to be accepted by Gaullist deputies who then fail to come) are not of any great use. There should be real debates and frank speaking on both sides. The results should be published. The principle of all discussions should be that it is not Franco-British relations which are under review but how best to avoid both our countries coming under the cultural, economic or political domination of either of the Super-Powers, subject always to our regarding the one as a friend and the other as a potential adversary.

Unless this criterion is accepted by both sides discussions are not likely to be productive. But why

should they not be? One would have thought that
the British and the French could have much to talk to
each other about on such a subject, and it must surely
be obvious by this time that it is no longer a question
of one country's trying to score points off the other.
Both are in a dangerous position, and will remain in
one until they can agree on how best to form
"Europe" with the participation of all the European
democracies and not only of some.

So it can be deduced, I suggest, that the second
British effort to join the EEC, though it may have
been mistimed and the determination of the great
adversary under-estimated, nevertheless did have a
good effect. For it demonstrated to most doubters that
Britain as a whole was sincere in her desire to throw
in her lot with Europe on the one condition that she
was not expected to be completely neutral as between
Russia and America—a condition which would be
warmly supported by the great bulk of public opinion
on the Continent, including a substantial section of
informed opinion in France.[2] But there would be fewer
doubters, and, after the necessary soundings, a final
effort would be more likely to succeed, if Her Majesty's
Government could make it clear that they favour
the gradual construction of a European Political Community employing the same techniques as those laid
down in the Treaty of Rome which, as we know, they
are prepared to abide by in its entirety. This idea will
be further developed in my conclusions.

[2] The "Association Française pour la Communauté
Atlantique," under the leadership of its very able Director,
Pierre Mahias, is doing excellent work in keeping alive in
France the general conception of the "Partnership."

7

Theory and Practice

AS HAS already been briefly suggested, it is quite possible to argue that the great European "Plan" of General de Gaulle was not something which existed in the sense of an objective that, one day, might actually be achieved, to the general satisfaction of Europeans, Russians, Americans and, indeed, the world as a whole. According to this school of thought, there was really no "Plan" of this sort at all, still less any precise indication of how this new "wider" European Union might be expected to work if it were ever constructed with Russia and without America and the United Kingdom: even the imposing slogan of "detente, entente and co-operation," always advanced as the "Open Sesame" for European consolidation, was, in practice, designed to allow France to pursue any policy that she believed was best suited to further her own interests in any particular circumstance. Thus she could at one moment hint at the advantages of the continued partition of Germany and at another emphasize the enduring value of the Franco-German Treaty for the purpose of achieving German reunification; sometimes celebrate the end of the Cold War, and sometimes side with Kosygin against America as in the Arab-Israel affair; now call on Great Power solidarity and now mobilize the smaller Powers under the leadership of France against the greater ones: in fact pursue from day to day totally contradictory policies. This is the conception of "movement," of "flexibility," of always irritating one "interlocutor" in order to curry favour with the other so as to be able at least to pull some chestnuts out of the fire, and then, before too much damage is done, suddenly switching round and finding an excellent reason for doing something totally different.

Take the idea—and it seems to be the idea—that it would be a good thing for the American armed forces to leave Germany so as to give France the opportunity of becoming the principal Western protector of the Federal Republic in accordance with the undisguised original intention of the Franco-German Treaty of January 1963. This could, under the "flexible" formula, be encouraged in various ways. France could either seek to persuade the Germans that, owing to the present exposed position of the American cities, the United States of America could never, in the event of a serious Russian challenge over Berlin, for example, be prepared to threaten nuclear action against the Soviet Union. Or she might suggest that the Americans, owing to their tremendous and growing power, are now much too rigid in their attitude and will therefore never be prepared to negotiate a German settlement, proposing rather to stay on indefinitely in Germany and thus perpetuate the *status quo*. Or she could at one and the same time insinuate both thoughts.

In general, this is the policy of "the game for the game's sake" which the intelligent Pierre Hassner thinks may have been the reason behind the General's more paradoxical attitudes.[1] We should no longer be surprised by these, he argues, if we realized that the idea was not to obtain any particular objective, but only to cut a dash and invariably put France in the centre of the stage. I myself had an inkling of this possible truth when in my recent book I wrote:

[1] Lecture to "*Association Indépendante des Sciences Politiques*," Brussels, September 1967.

"It is quite possible that we are all taking the recent attitudes of General de Gaulle too tragically ... Apparent contradictions or anomalies in French foreign policy cannot be taken at their face value. They are *tours de force*, designed to astonish the bourgeois, performed so far in perfect safety to a dazzled audience over the useful safety-net of American nuclear supremacy."[2]

On consideration, I would like to take back the bit about not taking them tragically: subsequent events have shown that we should take them very seriously. For if the performer crashes the result would not be pleasant for any of us; whereas if he consistently gets away with his exhibitions, other performers, probably less skilled, may appear on the tightrope too, which could be even more disastrous.

The point for examination, however, is whether, as Hassner says, we have to assume that de Gaulle's objective remained constant, but that his means of attaining it were absolutely flexible, or whether, on the contrary, the objective was variable while the means (i.e. "France first") were more or less constant. In other words, is there a case for thinking that the second interpretation is true, and that diplomatic action was simply an end in itself, the whole point of the exercise being to keep the pot boiling so that France could always bob up on top? There is, indeed, a case for so thinking and it rests on the idea that what was dominant in de Gaulle's thought was not

[2] *The European Idea*, Weidenfeld & Nicolson, 1966. Enlarged paper-back edition, New English Library, 1967, p. 76.

the original ideal of Europe itself which we quoted
at the beginning of this study (see pages 34 and
35) as the accompanying passage, which we have
also quoted, where he says that, whether the "Plan"
works or not, the point is that "France could take
effective action in this sense, play a splendid role,
and greatly further her own interests and those
of the human race." This judgment would, I feel,
on the whole be shared by the most acute if in some
respects the most sympathetic, of the critics of
Gaullist foreign policy, Professor Raymond Aron.[3]

If this interpretation is at all acceptable, it certainly
seems to follow that it is freedom of action which is
sought above all else and the consequent ability to
profit by the embarrassments and commitments of
others so as to achieve a dominating position for
France. This would be perfectly consistent, of course,
with the extreme importance which de Gaulle has
always attached to le rang, that is to say, to the status
of his country in the eyes of the world. So far as this
goes it is, indeed, consistent with the theory propounded before World War I, by Charles Maurras,
the violent French nationalist and inventor of the
theory of France seule.

Since we are necessarily basing ourselves chiefly on
written texts, we must here allude to the famous subsequent passage in de Gaulle's Mémoires which is more
global in its scope and reads as follows: "Seeing that
the collapse of Germany, the division of Europe, Russo-
American antagonism, provide France, miraculously
preserved, with exceptional possibilities for action, it

[3] "Guerre et Paix entres les Nations." Articles in Le
Figaro, passim.

occurs to me that the new period may, perhaps, allow me to set on foot the great plan which I have formed for my country. Guarantee security in Western Europe, by preventing a new Reich from threatening it once again. Collaborate both with the West and with the East, if necessary concluding with the one or with the other the appropriate alliance without ever accepting any kind of dependence ... Endeavour to group together, from the political, economic and strategic points of view, the States bordering on the Rhine, the Alps and the Pyrenees. Transform such an organization into one of the World Powers and one day, if necessary, the Arbiter between the Soviet and the Anglo-Saxon camps. Everything that I have done or said since 1940 has reflected such possibilities. Now that France has recovered her strength I shall try to give effect to them."[4]

It is a mistake not to take what the General writes as it were *ex cathedra* as an accurate indication of his thought. Sometimes this thought may be veiled, but in this case it is absolutely clear. The passage quoted was long meditated (and only revealed to the world in 1959) and there can be no doubt whatever that it means what it says. If we examine it carefully we see that the essential point is the emphasis on freedom of action for a France which—presumably at the head of a Western European "grouping" of states consisting of France, Germany, the Low Countries, Italy, Spain and (in theory) Switzerland—will be able to side now with the Americans and now with the Russians in order to dominate the world scene and if possible impose her own policy, that is to say in prac-

[4] Vol. III [*Le Salut*], p. 178.

tice French policy, on any particular issue. It is also absolutely clear that the British are regarded as a sort of American dependency. They are not, by definition, members of the proposed Western European "grouping," and they are undoubtedly included with the Americans under the term "Anglo-Saxon." We can therefore probably assume that "freedom of action" and "no dependence" is the major theme, and the formation of "Europe" (whether "from the Atlantic to the Urals" or in any other sense) the minor. That is to say, if by pressing "Europe," as he sees it, the General was able to keep France in the centre of the stage as an "equal" with the Super-Powers, he would press it; but if for this purpose it were preferable to adopt some other ploy then the "European" conception would be played down and pushed into the background.

Now if there is anything in this theory, one thing is clear: it is inconsistent with any policy directed towards establishing a durable, or even a transitory order in the world. For it must be obvious that as soon as the Super-Powers ever come to some agreement—if they ever do—the possibility for France to throw herself on the one side or the other disappears. Similarly if the Russians and the Germans were ever to come to some arrangement about Central Europe it would no longer be possible or desirable for either of them to invoke French assistance to achieve their end. And, finally, even if they were able to fix up such an arrangement by agreement with the French, and no doubt as a result of French services as an intermediary, no further opportunity would arise for profitable French intervention in the ensuing developments. Othello's occupation would be gone. Possibly in that event France might still be able to fling herself on the "Western" side, as suggested in the General's "vast plan"; but we must assume that the settlement in Europe would have been at least blessed by the Americans; for if it had not been, how could it, in practice, have come about except as the result of war? In other words, it would appear that, if the General is to be believed, nothing would suit France less than a general settlement. If we accept this reasoning it becomes abundantly clear why de Gaulle could never accept any form of "integration," that is to say something that might bind his hands, whether in an Atlantic or in a European context.

Looked at from another aspect, the policy can be compared to the Japanese art of Judo. Here the weaker party can often prevail over the stronger by, as it were, borrowing the latter's strength. France, by definition, is weaker than the two existing Super-Powers but she can defy them because she knows that, up to a certain point, they cannot, short of running a risk of general war, possibly employ all their strength. Moreover by her defiance she can win much approval on the part of the "developing" countries—who, individually, have virtually no power at all—and cannot themselves defy the Super-Powers. France, after all, is powerful. She can, in her own right, play a part in world monetary, economic and commercial affairs, and, thanks to the General, she will no doubt be able to play some part in nuclear affairs also. Hence, by deploying this power at a critical moment, and above all, in the right place, she can, as often as not, attain her immediate end and thus satisfy not only her own population but her own international clientèle. Only, in order to do this, she must possess complete freedom of action, for if she were tied to the one Super-Power or the other no such effective action would be possible.

But if this was the basic policy, two observations must be made. In the first place the game can only be played by a country whose leader has absolute command of foreign, and indeed of internal policy, and whose various moves are not subjected to effective scrutiny, still less criticism, in an elected Parliament, or even in a Council of Ministers. For if such a policy, as it must, contains a considerable element of bluff and of ruse, it cannot conceivably be explained in public without disaster. It would be rather as if Bismarck who, for a period at any rate, conducted a somewhat similar policy, had been obliged to explain to the Reichstag the full significance of the Ems telegram. Hence it was that General de Gaulle did not normally confide even in his closest associates before taking actions by which they were frequently just as surprised as the foreigners are, e.g. the recent embargo on the supply of French arms to Israel. *Ex post facto* justifications on television were all that was required, and television has indeed proved to be an ideal medium for putting across almost any policy to the French. The whole medium, as recent events have made manifest, was solely designed to further the ideas of *le Pouvoir*, and more especially its proposals as regards foreign affairs.

Thus, the French people can be constantly persuaded of the dreadful nature of American policy and semi-civilized conduct generally; of the instinctive desire of the British to sabotage the Common Market by entering it in a "Trojan Horse"; of the absolute necessity of spending huge sums on nuclear armaments rather than on education; or whatever is felt to be the most desirable note to strike at any given moment. Negatively too, the medium was of great importance. No attention need be directed to any criticism of Gaullist action by foreigners. On the contrary, every programme could be slanted to suggest that France, to the delight of all, was continuously progressing from strength to strength and making move after far-sighted move in the general interest of the human race. Above all, the actions of *le Pouvoir* could be equated with the actions of "France," which could be represented as above criticism as being, in a mystical way, the actions of all Frenchmen. Thus there was at the disposal of the Absolute Monarch— more absolute in some respects even than Louis XIV —a machine of which he could make excellent use in the application of his *secret du Roi*. Is it to be wondered at that he did his effective best to apply it? And, seeing that it often happened, in the pursuit of it, that France managed to score a point or two, perhaps it can be said that, for so long as it was pursued successfully, so much the better for France, if not for France's nominal friends and allies. After all, as the General once sagely remarked, "War is against one's enemies and peace is against one's friends."[5]

So to be successful this policy (if, indeed, it is the policy) must be conducted by an absolute ruler of great, if not indeed exceptional intelligence, courage and character. But there is another qualification, and it is a serious one. Even so pursued it can only be

[5] Tournoux, op. cit., p. 326.

successful if it is not challenged by another power of more or less equal strength which adopts a similar policy. It may, as Hassner says, be good for "the universe, as de Gaulle alleges, that France should always have free hands, but it is obviously not good for France if there are free hands for the universe." In less apocalyptic terms, there cannot be two *enfants terribles* in the world or, at the least, in the "Atlantic Community": they would inevitably cancel each other out. What might happen if the infection spread across the Channel is anybody's guess; happily at the moment it seems rather unlikely to do so. But it certainly is not difficult to see which other country might embrace the national philosophy of Charles Maurras and Charles de Gaulle. Across the Rhine there are already signs that some may be thinking, "Whatever de Gaulle can do, we can do better." And, indeed, why should not the Germans be tempted, in accordance with this formula, to "collaborate with the West and the East, if necessary, concluding with the one or with the other the appropriate alliances without ever accepting any kind of dependence"? It is quite true that, in order to do this successfully, the Germans would have to produce an inspired leader: but the Germans have been known to do just this in the past.

The answer of General de Gaulle would certainly be: "The Germans can do no such thing. They are cut in two and can therefore only have a broken-backed Government,[6] incapable of carrying out any really dynamic policy." But can one be quite sure? Might it not be possible to imagine some striking figure tak-

[6] Tournoux, op cit., p. 463.

ing command of Western Germany backed up by millions of enthusiastic young men and women, and going all out to conclude some kind of agreement with the Soviet Union which he could then, at his leisure, try to get round, or repudiate, the ultimate objective, though possibly veiled, always being clear—at least to him—namely German domination of Western Europe? The thought is an uncomfortable one, but the possibility should be faced. For the kind of nationalism practised by the late French Government, the "sacred egoism" so popular with some of the French, is undoubtedly catching. It was thus not very wise, perhaps, of the General, during his triumphal tour of Germany in 1962, to tell the German Military Academy in Hamburg that France and Germany had never accomplished anything great, from the national or international point of view, without their respective armed forces having been closely associated with it. Was it really necessary, when speaking to German soldiers, to invoke those spectres of the past, the French and the German invasions of Russia?

Finally, however, there is the reason put forward by Grosser namely that France is in a position to apply an opportunist policy of "prestige" and "grandeur" for the simple reason that she is France. Grosser evidently does not agree with this argument himself, but his description of it is well worth quoting.[7] "It should be noted, however," he says, "that Realpolitik has a limit. It applies to everyone except France. In describing his interview with President Truman, whom he finds to be a very mediocre man, de Gaulle explains

[7] Alfred Grosser: French Foreign Policy under de Gaulle, Little, Brown & Co., 1967.

that his welcome in the United States was very warm, not so much because he was General de Gaulle, but because of the '. . . extent of the city's extraordinary love of France.' I believe this is very important. All states are cold-blooded monsters, but *France is loved*. This is what justifies her receiving a special status not entirely independent of her power, but despite her lack of power. It is better that she should be powerful. More powerful, she will be more typically France. But even though not powerful, she benefits from a capital of affection in the world that no other country posses- ses, because no other country is France." And Grosser goes on to attribute this attitude to a kind of mar- riage which de Gaulle was able to effect between Jacobin ("left-wing") nationalism and the pure old- fashioned patriotism of the Right. On the whole, how- ever, it does not look as if this last justification of the policy of what might be called "prestige-opportun- ism" was very convincing. Love of France, indeed, however instinctive, is something which it is very difficult to reconcile with the policy of President de Gaulle.

What can be said of this policy is that its generaliz- ation would inevitably involve its collapse, and that it cannot succeed without being generalized. What is wanted in the common interest, therefore, is some- thing rather wider, something less cut-throat and desperate, in which all the countries of Western Europe at any rate can play a constructive and pre- arranged part. It is quite true that such a common policy can only be arrived at if all concerned agree to at least some measure of the detested "integration." But all save one of the countries concerned are willing to accept such measures. It is just not true to say that the United Kingdom is now unwilling to do so, nor is it fair to allege that certain members of the Six, and notably Germany, would be unwilling to go along with integration if it really came to the point. If, however, the "leader" of the European Economic Community refuses integration and three times in three years actually repudiates her solemn contractual obligations,[8] who is to encourage integrationist tendencies on the part of the Five? *Quis custodiet ipsos custodes*? Certainly not the European Court of Justice, so far as we can observe.

The tragedy is that many of the apparent objectives of Gaullist foreign policy—detente, general European settlement, etc.—would make sense if they were resolutely pursued by a unified Western Europe. But they cannot be achieved by a rogue elephant whose one idea is to increase the glory and the interests of his own country at the expense of the interests of everybody else, more especially those of his nominal allies. De Gaulle has been aptly called "the man of the day before yesterday and the day after tomorrow." We all know what he was in the first capacity: he was the *Grand Monarque*. But what would he be in his futuristic role? A World Federator? A new Charlemagne? The President of a European Union extending

[8] (1) Repudiation of Treaty obligation to accept "qualified" majority voting in Council of Ministers, on certain defined issues, by 1 January 1966 (violation of Article 148 of Treaty of Rome). (2) Refusal to allow negotiations on Britain's application to join EEC in 1967 (violation of Article 237). (3) Unilateral imposition of import controls without any consultation with partners in June 1968 (violation of Article 113).

to the Urals? It does seem rather difficult to see such a person emerging as the result of the tactics pursued, however successfully in the short run, by the late government of France.

Do we then conclude that what I have called a policy of "prestige-opportunism" was the key to de Gaulle's European policy? I think we can safely say, on the evidence available (a) that it was a very strong, perhaps the dominant, factor; (b) that it could only be pursued by a very exceptional, courageous and gifted man in absolute control of the political machine; (c) that it was highly dangerous, as leading to attempts to emulate it, and (d) that it was basically inconsistent with any constructive long-term European project. This is not to deny that the General's European "dream" may quite possibly have been sincerely held; but it ultimately represented a scheme for imposing French domination on a large section of the European Continent, not so much because France wanted to dominate anything as such, as because French "leadership" was essential in the interests of the human race. This brings us on to our general conclusions.

8

Conclusions

"WE MUST not be too hard on France for the trouble that she causes. For this country faces a cruel necessity. She has to take leave of that splendid ideology which has been her glory and her grandeur and whose many values have been generally recognized. The world would be the poorer if it lost the light which emanates from France... But what is now the issue is French insistence on treating that light as the sun which the whole universe must follow if it is not to lose its way. For so long as France persists in this attitude, the world will remain in that sad state of division which has become even more intolerable since the war: and for so long as she sticks to her nationalistic theories of yesterday and today she will be an obstacle to its evolution...

"France cannot read the signs of the times. She feels that the supremacy of her civilization is threatened; she observes that the peoples long ago freed themselves from her ascendancy; and she consequently believes that her national way of life [*forme*] is endangered. She remains true to herself in thinking that this way of life should be applicable to everybody ... [but] she cannot share the hope of reorganizing the world by international collaboration on a footing of equality. For eight centuries she exercised a hegemony. She strove for it, and defended it by every possible means. Her whole thought was penetrated by it. Her leaders never failed to tell her that the hegemony was not an unjustified ambition, but a logical consequence of the development of humanity. The whole reason for her existence has always been to be the first. Was this reason false? Could her 'voices' have lied? Impossible, she thinks, and that is why she can only view the prospect of a future not based on her hegemony as the suppression of her national existence.

"It is still from this angle that she contemplates the organization of the world. If France cannot lead then someone else will lead. So, must she accept the inevitable? Never! For years we have overheard this dialogue of contradictory voices. Never yet have we heard these voices coming together in a chorus which gives expression to the self-liberating theme: 'Nobody should dominate; nobody should be subjected; all must act together and collaborate with one another.'"

This is not a contemporary judgment. It was written forty years ago, before Nazism was invented, by a very pro-French, if rather vain and unreliable German called Friedrich Sieburg.[1] Some may feel that, if it was apposite in 1929, it is at least equally apposite today. Not so, I feel, many Frenchmen, and least of all their late President! It does, however, bring out rather vividly the essential differences between the Cartesian and the Hegelian approach to life and politics, and indeed the former is well represented by Bernard Grasset in a reply incorporated in the book itself. Is the present great dispute about how best to organize "Europe" a reflection of this difference? No doubt. Is there any means of overcoming it and arriving at some synthesis? We must all hope there is. But there can hardly be if the French continue to regard nationalist "grandeur" as the sole effective motive force in international politics, the only way to preserve the essentials of civilization and avoid, as it were, an

[1] *Dieu, est-il français?*, Bernard Grasset, 1930.

Umwertung aller Werter, a transmutation of all values. For by themselves, and in spite of their superb qualities, they are simply not now strong enough to impose their own preferred conception, even if they manage to continue for a time to do so by adopting the dazzling tactics of their erstwhile leader. Some new and generally accepted conception is consequently now required.

Let us start, therefore, with the simple belief of the heroic Nurse Cavell, inscribed on her statue in London opposite the Church of St Martin in the Fields, "Patriotism is not enough." This is something that everybody can understand and most accept. Have not two world wars proved its truth? But if it is not enough, what then? Do we pin all our hopes to the United Nations? One day the United Nations may represent a World State. More likely at the beginning of the next century—if our civilization survives this one—it may represent some valid World Authority. Even as things are, it represents the first, stumbling beginning of such an authority. But if it is to develop, the great political issues must first be solved, or at least some progress must be made towards their solution. America must somehow come to terms with the great emergent nations of the East, and, in the West, the Cold War must be ended. It is hardly for Europeans to give unwanted advice to the Americans on the first great issue. Britain is no longer "present" in the Far East in an effective military sense, and, whatever the Tory party may now say, it is unlikely that if she remains outside "Europe" she will have any military presence there at all after 1972—or, for that matter, in other parts of the Indian Ocean area. But the second issue is one in which Britain and her European neighbours are vitally involved. For it concerns that still potential source of World War III, namely the division of the Continent and the future of the German people.

There are those who maintain that the right approach to this tremendous problem, anyhow for the British, is to forget about "Europe" altogether and concentrate on increasing trade by some widespread "Free Trade Area" embracing to start with the United States, Canada, the United Kingdom and Australasia and perhaps one or two members of EFTA, but open to any other industrialized country, above all, Japan, and even, one day, the EEC itself. But unless it is conceived of as having some political content, this idea would probably in practice reduce itself to the encouragement of a further "Kennedy Round" of tariff-cutting or the abolition of the real present impediments to free trade, such as the "voluntary" restrictions on many Japanese exports to the great American and indeed to the European markets. This would be an excellent thing and it is greatly to be hoped that every effort will be made to achieve it. Presumably also such efforts to liberate trade would cover such matters as freedom on the part of those concerned to invest capital in each others' countries to say nothing of freedom of migration. But if it does have a political content—and it would if it meant forming a *bloc* which would discriminate by tariffs against non-members—it means contemplating some political union of the "Anglo-Saxons" to start off with which might eventually be extended to other great industrialized countries—a sort of incipient World State, to be formed, it would appear, *before* we have solved the two fundamental political problems of our era to which I have already alluded.

A political union of the "Anglo-Saxons" may indeed be something into which we may be driven if "Europe" is ever established on French lines, which is no doubt unlikely, or if—perhaps as the result of Soviet military threats—it is not formed at all and the Germans consequently come to terms on their own with the Russians. But in either eventuality the chances of enduring peace would be gravely prejudiced, the world situation becoming even more explosive than at present. For the short point is that even if an "Atlantic Free Trade Area" were formed and achieved some basic political content it would not solve the problem of German reunification; it would only intensify the Cold War and the confrontation of the Super-Powers on the Elbe. Few people who are really capable of thinking in political terms at all should consequently favour such a plan, whatever its theoretical economic advantages. In any case, it is unlikely for fairly obvious protectionist reasons to be encouraged by any prospective American administration. What is quite clear is that the subject of this essay would claim that attempts by the British government to move in this direction entirely proved his point, namely that Britain is not really concerned with "creating Europe," but is only out to "organize a colossal Atlantic Community under the influence and direction of America which would make short work of absorbing the European Community."[2] This

[2] Press Conference of 14 January 1963.

would naturally be most unfair, seeing that de Gaulle, and only he, was responsible for the exclusion of Britain from "Europe," but there is no doubt that the allegation would be effective.

It has, I know, been suggested by certain great authorities, notably by Sir Robert Scott,[8] that the advantage of some kind of "NAFTA" would be to enable the United Kingdom to continue, or resume, an independent military role in the Far East and the area of the Indian Ocean. It is difficult to see how this could be achieved by a country which has now acquired such a mountainous debt, even if economic circumstances should be improved by entering some Anglo-Saxon trading *bloc*, which is perhaps questionable. If it is economically possible, there is, of course, a strong case for a continuing British military role of some kind in the area concerned, though probably only if it is based on Australia with communications passing over the New World and the Pacific and not over a hostile Middle East and a largely hostile Africa. But an "independent" role is probably only conceivable if the British manage to get the "Europeans" interested in it and make it a joint effort largely based on combined French and British naval and air power. To think that the British are now capable by themselves of undertaking such a role is, I fear, probably the last of their ex-Imperial delusions. It is only now, by strengthening their base, that they can eventually become more "outward-looking," as Scott always has it. It is only "Europe," if formed, that from now on, if it should ever so decide, can take up again to some extent the previous stabilizing role of the old French

[8] Atlantic Trade Study, July 1968.

and British "civilizing missions," or, as we used to say, the White Man's Burden.

So we come to the same inevitable point. If we are to avoid major dangers, we must construct some European entity comprising all European industrialized and democratic countries: if such a construction is to come about, France will have to change her present nationalistic policies. If the patient reader has followed the argument of this little book at all, it is to be hoped that he, too, will have arrived at this first conclusion. But, if so, then another immediately presents itself. If the nationalistic conceptions of France will not result in a united Europe, neither will such nationalistic conceptions if they are adopted by the United Kingdom. For if such a Union is unlikely to be based on one hegemony, it is quite impossible that it should be based on two. The "mot" attributed to Edgar Pisani is entirely valid: one cock, five hens very good, two cocks, five hens, hopeless.

Therefore, from the outset, both France and Britain must be prepared to accept certain supra-national obligations. There is no other way. Have the British accepted this non-Gaullist philosophy? Probably not, at any rate consciously. For the British are not inclined to accept any political philosophy: they merely hope that, somehow, they will muddle through. Nevertheless at some point the British government does have to take decisions involving great questions of principle. Twice they have sought to enter the European Economic Community, which, if the Treaty of Rome is to be taken seriously at all, is a supra-national organization. All British parties are in principle committed to approval of this form of society. In 1962 and again in 1967, both the Tory and the Labour Governments explicitly said that they accepted the political implications of the Common Market, now repudiated, as we all know, by General de Gaulle. But has the point yet been made sufficiently clear?

It has not: and it should be. If indeed we believe (a) that "Europe" should somehow be united; (b) that we should be in it, and (c) that it should not be united under the hegemony of any one country, then it should make it clear what exactly is the sort of Europe that the British should wish to join and which they shall explicitly work towards if they do join. Otherwise they really do have very little to say in reply to the Gaullist suggestion that the only reason why they want to come into the Community is to break it up and turn it into a "colossal Free Trade Area," depriving it, in other words, of any real political content. It is quite true that the political content which the Gaullist government contemplated is one which is unlikely to result in a genuine union; but at least it was a form of political content. Also the British have a good deal to live down, so far as Europe is concerned. Those who have followed the narrative in this small work will not indeed be surprised to hear that many people in the countries of the EEC still suspect their motives. It is for them, therefore, not only to go on saying that they want to join the EEC—as the government rightly does—but also to make clear that, once in, they would abide by the Treaty of Rome, including acceptance of the prescribed role of the Commission; of majority voting where so provided in the Treaty; and of supervisory powers of a Parliament that would eventually be directly elected; and, in addition, work for the early establishment of a Political Community which would gradually apply much the same techniques in the field of foreign policy and defence as well.

One would have thought that, having come so far along the "European" road the British government would not shrink at some suitable moment from thus nailing their colours to the mast: nor should they have much trouble with their supporters if they did so. Certainly they should not have any serious trouble with the Opposition. What they would, however, be making clear—and it would have an immensely encouraging effect on the Continent if they did make it clear—would be that, in their view, the nationalistic philosophy was not a viable basis for the construction of "Europe," and that in any case it was not one which they themselves could or would accept. If it proves anything, the Russian rape of Czechoslovakia proves that the West Germans cannot carry out their laudible *Ostpolitik* with the sole assistance of France. For if there ever is to be a real detente—and the entire *Ostpolitik* is based on this possibility—it can only be achieved by the formation in Western Europe of some entity, embracing the United Kingdom, which will enable the Americans to withdraw their forces to their homeland on condition that the Russians do the same. Short of this there is at least a shadow of substance in the Russian equation of detente with the disruption of the "Socialist bloc." And it stands to reason that such a Western Europe cannot emerge unless its component parts accept at least some supra-national disciplines. What are the chances of such a philosophy being accepted by the government of France?

Well, if our enquiry shows anything it is that the General would rather die—that is to say, he would rather that France died—than accept anything of the kind.

But he has gone, and he will very probably be followed, not by anarchy—as he always so confidently predicted—but by some reasonable, democratic politician who will rally the nation and keep it within the circle of the great Western European democracies. The "Great Anarch," in other words, may have let the curtain fall, but we can be pretty sure that Georges Pompidou or Alain Poher, or some other solid republican character will now rush out and catch it. The question is, will the new leader be tempted, or will he be able to carry on the European policy of General de Gaulle?

There are those who maintain that he can and he will: that de Gaulle's nationalistic theses, shorn no doubt of their idiosyncrasies and their intolerable style, respond to the basic instincts of the French people as described in the quotation at the beginning of this Chapter. In other words, that the whole idea of supra-nationality is so alien to the French nation that, even if it is accepted intellectually by French statesmen, it is inevitably in the long run repudiated in practice by the hard-headed French bourgeois with his heart on the left and his pocket-book on the right. Such people—and they include many who know France well—would point to the repudiation, in 1954, of the European Defence Community—originally prepared by French theoreticians—and by the refusal of France in 1965 to stand by the majority voting provisions in the Treaty of Rome in the drafting of which French specialists had likewise taken the lead.

There is some truth in this analysis. But we must remember that the explosion of French nationalism which resulted in the rejection of the EDC could not prevent the rearmament of the Western Germans and the subsequent establishment of WEU. Nor did the French repudiation of the Treaty of Rome in 1965 actually destroy the supra-national establishment in Brussels; it only weakened it, and it is still very much alive. What is quite certain is that an entirely nationalist policy cannot be conducted by any successor with the same vigour and effectiveness as it was conducted by General de Gaulle. Even if there is still a nationalist President and a nationalist majority in the French Assembly the combination is not now likely to give very coherent and unchallenged expression to nationalist ideals. Strong opposition from various political groups who favour the alternative policy of progressing with the construction of "Europe" within the framework of the Western Alliance will not now be able to be suppressed or to be deprived of television facilities. The Assembly, too, is much more likely now to assert itself. In the nature of things, much power will probably pass from the Presidential Elysée to the Prime Ministerial Matignon. Nor should we altogether dismiss the prophecy of the General himself that once he had turned his back Britain will be in the Common Market![4]

But the point is that progress towards the formation of a genuine European Community, though it

[4] Tournoux, op. cit., p. 464.

will still be slow and difficult is now at least possible. The various nationalist forces that exist in all the countries concerned will no longer now be able, as it were, to hide behind the General, and that is a good thing because the great issue can now be fought out on more realistic terms. In Britain, for instance, the Government would be well advised, pending the initiation of negotiations for British entry into the Common Market—which even on the most optimistic assumptions could probably not occur until after the German elections in the autumn—to come out with schemes for co-operation in many spheres outside the Treaty of Rome and to cause them to be discussed either in the WEU or outside it. It seems unlikely that the new French Government would actually boycott the discussion of such schemes. Why should it? Even if—as is to be hoped—such schemes contained a considerable supra-national element, it would seem inevitable that any new democratic French Government should at least discuss them with France's friends and allies. If nationalism in Britain—which, after all, is quite possibly as strong as it is in France—can be contained, in other words, why should it not be contained across the Channel?

It is, I know often alleged that the British have no policy. That, stunned by the disappearance of the Commonwealth and Empire, they are marking time, thinking only of their balance of payments and their standard of living, becoming increasingly introspective, not to say provincial, in short that they have, nearly a quarter of a century after the great victory in which they had so proud a share, lost their way, become rather defeatist, and not yet found their role. This is an exaggerated picture but there does seem to be some truth in it. Britain is as often as not ignored in the great debates that convulse America, the Middle East, the Far East and the continent of Europe. Her envoys are insulted, her embassies burnt, her tail is twisted by General Franco, her few remaining colonies appear to be up for disposal. Even the possibility of the secession of Scotland and Wales is solemnly discussed. Not since Admiral van Tromp sailed up the Medway does there seem to have been such a failure of the national purpose and will, though it must be remembered that shortly after this distressing episode England entered into a very glorious period in her history. But how are they to snap out of the present mood and recover some assurance of where they are going and what exactly they intend to do?

By coming out for "Europe" in the sense just suggested, but, more importantly, by saying why exactly, from the long-term point of view, they want to form a European Political Community. Oddly enough, this should be for many of the reasons given in favour of the construction of "Europe" by General de Gaulle, who, if only he had followed his reason and not his ancestral "voices," would have been by this time the first virtual President of Europe instead of (as Senator de la Vallée Poussin observed at the December 1967 meeting of the Western European Union Assembly) the "last of the great Ministers of Louis XIV." For it is entirely reasonable that "Europe," that is to say those nations which have always formed what has come to be known as Western Civilization, in other words the countries West of the Soviet border, should try jointly to recover the influence which they once had in the world. Nothing could promote the cause of world peace more than the creation of such an entity which could interpose itself between the two giants and enable them to abandon the ever-dangerous "confrontation" on the Elbe. There undoubtedly is a basic understanding between the races of this "Europe," in the sense of a desire for a certain type of society and of government which we can call "democratic" for want of a better description. For it is, indeed, the home and the origin of the kind of civilization which has now spread over most of the world.

But where Britain could never follow the General —any more than the bulk of Western Europeans could follow him either—was in his insistence that this "Europe" must be nearer to Russia than to America, nearer, that is to say to a great nation which has never been more than partially penetrated by Western values and which has never experienced anything approaching liberal or social democracy. In a word, which has never known what freedom is and has always, when she could, suppressed it. Further, too, from another great nation which, however much it may be criticized and whatever its internal difficulties and struggles, has a political system based on freedom and which in any case, as the General himself has said, is, as it were, the "Daughter of Europe"? It really is not a question of Europe, if it is ever formed, becoming submerged in an alien culture; it is a question of the Mother and the Daughter living together on terms of mutual respect, each with her own responsibilities, and working in effective partnership the exact nature of which could be gradually elaborated.[5]

The General would probably maintain that such sentiments have nothing to do with what he calls "reality," in other words, what is usually known as *Realpolitik*. Under his policy, as we have seen, if America appears to be stronger than Russia, "Europe" (which, at the moment, is only France) must throw herself on the side of the "weaker" power in order to preserve the "balance." If Europe were ever formed in a political sense it is evident that it would have the possibility of so acting if it so desired; but what is almost inconceivable is that it would be able, or indeed would want, to have "free hands" in the sense analysed in Chapter 7. True, it would have to work out its own defence policy, but it is obvious that for a considerable time it could hardly afford to be altogether independent of the United States. The great thing is to form it: and it cannot ever be formed if, as a first prerequisite, all the governments concerned have to declare that in all respects they share the foreign political objectives, whatever they may be, of the Government of France.

There was another unacceptable feature of the General's policy—unacceptable, that is, to Britain, and probably to his partners in the EEC. This was, of course, his insistence on the absolute independence and inviolate sovereignty of all members of the Community. In practice, as we have seen, this means

[5] This has been, and still is, the thesis of Mr George Ball whose recent admirable book, *The Discipline of Power* (Bodley Head, 1968) should be read by all those interested in the future of Europe.

absolute independence for France, the others being expected to follow her lead if only because of her history,
her place on the map, and her great civilizing traditions. If one thing is certain, it is that if we came in,
this particular method of arriving at some form of
European unity could not possibly work; and this,
apart from our initial mistakes and missed oppor-
tunities, is the sole reason why we have so far been
excluded. What is meant by "working"? If you hold
with the General, and indeed with such distinguished
scholars as Professor Stanley Hoffmann[6] of Harvard
that in the foreseeable future the only conceivable basis
for any kind of international order is the sovereign
Nation-State; that a struggle between these entities
for power and influence is an elementary fact of life;
and that there is no particular prospect of this state
of affairs changing, anyway during the present century, then you can argue that, if "Europe" ever
emerges as a political unit, it can only be as a result
of some struggle between France, Germany and
Britain. But even if this rather desperate philosophy
is acceptable it seems, to say the least, likely that any
such internecine struggle would only result in a great
extension of the influence of one or the other of the
Super-Powers, or more probably, of both. The truth
surely is that, whether we like it or not, we are in a
period in which so far as the heavily industrialized

[6] *Gulliver's Troubles*, McGraw-Hill, 1968. On p. 406
of this admirable, if rather gloomy, work Professor Hoffmann says that "the Nation State remains indefinitely
the centre of aspirations and calculations." On p. 412
et seq. he demonstrates how the ensuing situation, so far
as Europe is concerned, must inevitably result in absolute
deadlock.

nations are concerned, large regional groupings are being formed: and, if they are formed, the states which compose them must lose part of their entire freedom of action.

We therefore arrive at our final conclusion. The European policy of de Gaulle, if consistent, was inoperable; if operable, inconsistent. If we believe at all in the formation of "Europe" we must stand out for the opposite conception of a genuine Community governing itself and not being governed by the play of various unpredictable national wills. If we do stand out for this and simply await our opportunity, not being distracted from our objective by other schemes, we shall win through in the end. And in so doing we shall bury the hatchet with France, just as the General has buried it, or half-buried it, with Germany. Once, indeed, Britain does join the EEC there will be no European hatchets left to bury. We must, therefore, not only oppose any schemes based on de Gaulle's conceptions, but constantly vaunt the advantages of our own very different European convictions. If we are to vaunt them we must first believe in them. And what else is there now left in which we can believe?

As for the tragic, tremendous figure of the General, it is certain that it will go down in French history as the saviour of his country in her hour of need, and that is no doubt what he most desires. But his tragedy was that he has, in pursuing his great enterprises, usually achieved the opposite of what he apparently wanted, and that in always saying "No" he inevitably provoked an ultimately deafening and triumphant "Yes." His own Boswell sums it all up as follows:[7]

[7] Tournoux, op. cit., p. 471.

"The General's life can best be described as the quintessence of permanent contradiction. The eternal paradox that possesses him leads de Gaulle to turn his back on Europe and yet to promote it in the nature of things; to foster nationalisms and to stimulate the birth of a European patriotism; to push back the English towards the Ocean and to confirm Great Britain in her intention to bind herself to the Continent." As an epitaph on his European policy, which it has been the object of this essay to assess, we cannot improve on that. That de Gaulle is a great and overwhelming personality, who in many respects has promoted the short-term interests of his country, no one can doubt. That he has pursued a European policy which, in the nature of things, must be contested by any British Government, is obvious. That this policy will never result in a united Europe is most probable. That unless at least a united Western Europe is formed both his country and ours will fairly shortly lose all real freedom of action is certain. These are the conclusions to which any objective British study of his European policy must surely point. It is therefore greatly to be hoped that, for one reason or another, such a policy will not be pursued by France for very much longer. But it must be hoped that Great Britain, too, will explicitly reject the Gaullist nationalist thesis, and likewise agree to replace it by the broad conception of a valid European Authority. For only in such a framework can those old friend-enemies, La France et l'Angleterre, unite their strengths for the benefit, not only of Europe, but of all humanity.

Glossary of Abbreviations

(relating to international organizations with some
bearing on European matters)

BENELUX *Customs Union* between the three Low
Countries concluded in 1948. Now virtually merged in
EEC (q.v.).

CERN *European Organization for Nuclear Research.*
Set up in 1952 to provide for collaboration among European
countries in fundamental nuclear research. Not concerned
with work for military purposes. Membership:
Austria, Belgium, Denmark, France, Western Germany,
Greece, Italy, Netherlands, Norway, Spain, Sweden,
Switzerland, United Kingdom and Yugoslavia.

COM ECON The *"Committee for Mutual Economic
Assistance".* Set up by the Russians as a kind of equivalent
to the EEC in Eastern Europe. Differs from the EEC
in that the USSR also attempts to organize industries in
the member States.

C. of E. *Council of Europe.* Consists at present of 18
States, namely the EEC (q.v.), the EFTA (q.v.) (less Portugal).
Iceland, Cyprus, Malta, Ireland, Greece and Turkey.
Committee of Ministers proceeds by unanimity on all
important matters; Assembly has interesting, but inconclusive
debates; Secretariat, under the Ministers, patiently
elaborates useful conventions on secondary matters of
common interest that usually only come into force after
long delays. Human Rights section is important and
European Human Rights Convention is functioning satisfactorily,
save only in France.

ECE *Economic Commission for Europe.* Founded under
UN auspices in post-war period before Cold War
developed. Consists of all countries in geographical Europe
plus the USA. Largely a survival from pre-Cold War days.
Useful activities are small and tend to vary with progress
or regress of "Detente".

ECSC *European Coal and Steel Community.* First
successful effort (1951) towards European integration, as
opposed to association. Members, same as EEC (q.v.).
Firmly based on supra-national principle. Includes "High
Authority" and Parliament. Now proposed to merge it
with EEC, but merger not yet definitely effected.

EDC *European Defence Community.* Was supposed to constitute the next great step towards full European political integration, but was rejected by French Parliament in 1954 and collapsed. The UK at first gave the impression that it might join but then ran out.

EEC *European Economic Community.* ("The Six") The great triumph of the European Federalists after the defeat of the EDC. Came into force on 1 January 1958. Members, France, Germany, Italy and the Low Countries. Has achieved common external tariff and common agricultural policy. Supra-national element strongly challenged by Gaullist Government who are still working for a simple Customs Union under French hegemony. Parliament (which has little influence) not yet directly elected. Only hope of survival as Economic and (potentially) a Political Union probably lies in extension so as to include a UK converted to supra-national principle.

EFTA *European Free Trade Association.* Consists of those Western European States, namely UK, Norway, Denmark, Sweden, Austria, Switzerland and Portugal, which (in 1958) could not take the EEC. Founded in 1959 as a sort of riposte to latter. Tariffs on industrial products now virtually abolished as between members (save Portugal). Has greatly facilitated and stimulated trade but all members now hope for eventual join up with EEC. This has so far been prevented by the Gaullists.

ELDO *European Launcher Development Organization.* Founded in 1962. Was supposed to create a "European" Rocket that would put "Europe" into the space race. But as "Europe" has not been formed project seems to be petering out and UK is now gradually withdrawing. Members, all industrialized Western European States (including Spain) plus Australia.

EPC *European Political Community*, sometimes known as "Fourth Community". This does not exist but if Gaullists continue to exclude Britain from the EEC it may possibly be formed among those European States who object to such exclusion. It would, in principle, cover all fields not covered by Treaties of Rome setting up EEC and EURATOM. If formed, object would be to merge it with EEC as soon as possible.

ESRO *European Space Research Organization.* Still surviving, and doing useful work. Members as in ELDO with exception of Australia.

EURATOM The "*Third Community,*" the others being EEC and ECSC. In principle, to be merged with other two, but is in a bad way, chiefly owing to the attitude of France.

GATT *General Agreement on Tariffs and Trade.* Functioning since 1947. Based on Most Favoured Nations principle and still the basis of international trade. Members, all non-Communist industrialized States (together with Yugoslavia and Czechoslovakia) plus some of the more important under-developed—about fifty in all. Threatened by growth of protectionism and regional blocs.

"GREATER EUROPE" Term of art indicating ultimate ideal of union of all European States west of the Russian frontier. Often employed by anti-Europeans to delay or prevent unity in Western Europe only.

"LITTLE EUROPE" Pejorative term employed to denote union of EEC (q.v.) countries only. Sometimes used to denote anything less than "Greater Europe" (see above).

NAA *North Atlantic Assembly.* Semi-official gathering of Parliamentarians from NATO countries, now centred in Brussels.

NAFTA *North Atlantic Free Trade Association.* Proposal backed chiefly by those who do not wish Britain to join the EEC. Not as yet definitely formulated—i.e. would it, in principle, include only "North Atlantic" countries or be all embracing? Difficult to reconcile with continued existence of EEC. Unlikely to be accepted by the USA.

NATO *North Atlantic Treaty Organization.* Based on, but to be distinguished from, North Atlantic Treaty of 1949 (which can be denounced by any member after 1969). No longer includes France. Membership: 12 Western and Southern European nations plus USA and Canada. In practice, based on "integration" or armed forces under American leadership (contains no supra-national element). Considered by all, save France, to be essential in default of German settlement.

OECD Organization for European Cooperation and Development. Took over in 1959 from OEEC (see below) and does much useful work in coordinating western economic policies and in trying to elaborate a common policy as regards under-developed countries. Members, all non-Communist European States plus USA, Canada and Japan.

OEEC Organization for European Economic Cooperation. Formed in 1948 to organize Marshall Aid to European countries under permanent British chairmanship. With conclusion of EEC in 1958 and subsequent collapse of general European Free Trade plan, faded out and was replaced by OECD (q.v.).

WARSAW PACT Set up in 1955 as a "Treaty of Friendship, Cooperation and Mutual Assistance" between the USSR, Albania, Bulgaria, East Germany, Hungary, Poland, Roumania and Czechoslovakia. Always represented by Russians as the equivalent of NATO, but in fact represents the Russian Empire rather than an Alliance from which any member can legally withdraw, though Albania has, in practice, revolted and joined China.

WEU Western European Union. Founded in 1954 after collapse of EDC (q.v.) largely with object of legalizing German rearmament. Consists of Six plus UK. Its Assembly is a useful forum, but Council of Ministers does not work, chiefly owing to lack of French cooperation. Non supra-national. If French policy changes, might form basis of supra-national EPC (q.v.).

Index